THAT LITTLE GIRL HAS A MIND OF HER OWN

The tales of a precocious child growing up in a different time

Foreword

I was that little girl who laid on her back in the soft grass, imagining that the fluff of white clouds was a parade of circus elephants, marching trunk to tail, or a giant gray white fish, with fins and gills, swimming in the blue sky ocean. I was that little girl, with mason jars filled with lightning bugs on her window sill. I was that little girl who wrapped herself in the folds of her grandmother's housecoat and listened for hours to countless stories of swashbuckling pirates, fairy princesses, and my grandmother's recollection of things past. I have chronicled those stories and stories of my own, hoping that those of a certain age will remember, and those much younger will have a better understanding of how things used to be.

M H King

Chapter One

And so My Story Begins—as told to me by my mother

The shrill cries of a newborn echoed down the cold, dark, nearly empty hallways of the maternity ward. Much like the unsettling buzzing and beeping of an alarm clock, letting the nursery staff know that they had a new arrival. Up until this time, it had been a rather sleepy night. Now the silence had been interrupted by the rustling of starchy white uniforms and the squishy sound of rubber soled nurses' shoes scurrying down the corridor to delivery room 2B.

A baby's arrival was, by no stretch of the imagination, an unusual occurrence. After all, this was a hospital and this was the maternity ward. So why all the excitement? As it turned out, the woman who had just delivered her first child was also the newest member of the delivery room staff.

She had quickly made friends since her arrival three months prior and it hadn't taken long for her to gain the respect of her peers. She was hardworking, smart, quick to take charge, and fun to be around. She was particularly popular with the team of doctors who appreciated her confident demeanor and her work ethic. I'm also sure that it didn't hurt that she was very attractive. She was tiny and her pregnancy had gone mostly unnoticed under her blousy uniform. So, when she finally revealed her baby bump, everyone was very surprised and anxious for the birth.

Back in the day, soon-to-be fathers were relegated to a tiny, way too well-lit room on the periphery of the action. That's where my dad huddled with the other sailors waiting for their moment of introduction. It turned out to be quite a long wait, for more often than not, babies (especially first babies) are in no rush to leave the comfort of a warm, watery womb. I was no exception. At precisely 0755, I made my first appearance. Born kicking and most assuredly screaming, I had arrived.

It was 1944, and my father had been called up by Uncle Sam to fight in the war of all wars. To be sure, he was no John Wayne. He had no testosterone-exaggerated vision of going to Europe and doing hand to hand combat with Adolf Hitler. He was raised, however, with a strong obligation to God and country. When he was sent to the Navy Air Base in Norman, Oklahoma to train tail gunners, it was an assignment that he was all too happy to pack up his duffle bag for. Thank goodness, it kept him stateside.

My mother had tagged along, not wanting to be away from her new husband. They had married just eleven months before my birth and being in their early twenties were just getting used to the whole marriage bit. Now they had a baby.

After the mandatory five post-delivery days in the hospital, my mom dressed me in scads of things girly pink and wrapped me in a soft, even pinker, receiving blanket for the trip home. The proud Papa pulled up to the hospital's side entrance, piled his family into an old yellow, bleached from the sun, Ford station wagon and headed to where the enlisted men and their families were housed.

Home was just outside the confines of the huge, sprawling naval-air base. Rows and rows of like colored bungalows provided shelter for the scores of military families that were temporarily ensconced there. There were few trees, no flowering bushes and not much of anything that looked like home. It was nothing like my mother's house in Elmira, New York, where hundred-year-old elms and chestnuts lined the streets.

Clouds of chocolate brown dust whirled behind our car as we pulled up in front of the house. A small stoop stuck out of the front like an afterthought. It was your basic box with windows. Inside was unremarkable as well. The tiny kitchen had appliances that had seen a better day and hideous maroon, organdy curtains that were probably the rage during the last world war. The living room was furnished with an overstuffed sofa and matching armchair. Both of which were much too scratchy to sit on. My parents had placed a small bassinet in the corner of the living room that had been designated as my nursery. I was home.

My parents had thought that they were prepared for their new addition, but this proved to be a serious error in judgement. I was a very, very cranky baby. Not cuddly, not cute, not chubby and most certainly not cooperative. I didn't eat. I didn't sleep. The one thing that I did do well was cry. I screamed, whined, wailed, and sobbed. I was a handful. When my parents' friends came to check out the new arrival, most of them left quickly after stating the obligatory, "What a cute baby." To be assured, I was not by any stretch of the imagination, "cute".

Though I was full term at birth, I tipped the scale at less than six pounds. Just imagine, a newborn with long scrawny legs and a kidney shaped head, a bit elongated from spending too many hours in the birth canal. Add to that, an excessive amount of jet-black hair that covered, not only my misshapen head, but the rest of my tiny body as well. Think little girl spider monkey. One of my dad's sailor friends, after a brief but bellowing introduction, signed my baby book as such, "That little girl has a mind of her own."

Alas, my parents were plunged into the cranky world of babydom. There were way too many sleepless nights and far too few tranquil days. Our small space was jam packed with baby paraphernalia intended to make their little girl coo like the Gerber baby on the box of oatmeal. That, unfortunately, did not happen. Babies that don't eat are sure to be cranky, and I refused to eat.

Weeks went by and when strained baby food was introduced, I remained the reluctant eater. If, by some miracle, a bit did get into my mouth, it was ejected either with a quick spit or a slower more deliberate dribble down the front of my terry cloth bib. Strained carrots, peas, applesauce, and pears had no allure. The strained spinach was particularly gross and disgusting. I had no intention of ingesting a food that was the color of green slime.

I cried and cried and cried.

Chapter Two
An Ill Wind Blowing—recounted to me by my mother

When a friend of my mother's telephoned and invited us to come visit for the day, Mom was all too eager to accept her invitation. They had met several months prior, when my mother first arrived in Norman, but soon after, she had been transferred to a hospital in Tulsa. Tulsa was just a two-hour train ride away, so the following week, we packed up and headed to the railroad station.

It was a typical spring day when we left the house. The sky was a tad overcast, with a chance of showers. But nothing that was going to dampen Mom's excitement of seeing her friend, showing off her new baby, and most importantly, "getting out of Dodge" for the day.

We arrived with plenty of time to spare, but mom still scurried to the ticket window, not wanting to miss the train. At precisely nine o'clock, the giant chunk of metal lumbered into the depot, spewing watery vapor the color of an angry gray sky from its massive cylindrical smokestacks. Puffs of pearly charcoal smoke took the form of enormous earthbound cumulus clouds. The passengers on the platform disappeared into a London-like fog of coal smoke and steam. After a squealing of metal on metal, the train came to a stop and the crowd of travelers began to pour into the waiting cars.

We were confronted by a sea of shiny shaved heads. On this day, the military was definitely traveling by land. Mom staggered, under the weight of her load, as she balanced

9

me on one hip and the quintessential diaper bag on the other. She trudged down the crowded aisles searching desperately for a space for her and her precious cargo. When she had all but given up, she saw a seat near the back of the train that she thought might have potential. As she approached, the two burly marines that occupied the space, obligingly motioned that they would make room. After some maneuvering, we were at last smooshed into a space that truly wasn't one. There I was, juxtaposed between my mother and a complete stranger on my first excursion into the real world.

The ride was uneventful for the first hour or so. Mom sat staring straight ahead with me clutched tightly to her chest. Aside from the cordial hello, good morning, there was no conversation with her seat mates.

Without so much as a warning, the sunlight that had been streaming into our car, had conspicuously disappeared and been replaced by an eerie darkness that put the train's conductor immediately on edge. Suddenly, everything became very quiet, an uncomfortable kind of quiet that made my mom hold me even tighter.

Then there was wind. Wind that roared and pushed and made a weird whirling sound. Wind that was powerful and angry. Wind that began to rock the train like a hobby horse on Christmas morning. The conductor mustered his most commanding voice as he ordered us to crawl under our seats, but the space was terribly confining.

Pandemonium had swept over the train as the violent shaking continued. The pressure of the wind was actually pushing on the windows, bowing them in and out as if they were taking their last breath. There was, at that moment, a terrible pop in the front of the car and it immediately filled with dirt and sand and everything caught up in the turbulence. This was, by no stretch of the imagination, just your average spring storm. We were caught up in the unimaginable violence of a tornado.

Everyone was scared to death. The noise was deafening. My mother was not her usual cool and collected self and I didn't at all care for huddling on the floor in a space that was usually reserved for soldiers' boots. I began to fuss and after fuss there was cry and after cry, there was scream. The young hulk of a marine who was crouched next to my mother could finally take no more. It seemed as if my crying was immensely more annoying than the roar of the tornado. He motioned to my mother to hand me over and she more than willingly obliged. He unzipped his jacket and tucked me feet first into the cavernous wooly lining. I stopped crying and exhausted, fell fast asleep. This is where I rode out the remainder of the storm.

As quickly as the tornado had struck, it was gone. It disappeared in a funnel of chaotic energy, whirling across the desert landscape, as if it was late for its own demise. The train full of bewildered passengers had begun to cautiously return to the present and somehow come to grips with what had just happened. Luckily, no one was seriously hurt, just a few bumps, bruises and minor cuts from broken glass. Everyone breathed a consensual sigh of relief as an omnipresent calm pushed fear from the disheveled car and its unwitting passengers. Help arrived and quickly transferred all aboard to another train, and we proceeded onto our destination. Almost none the worse for wear.

I spent the remainder of the day, relaxing with Mom and her friend, curled up like a little chipmunk in my nest of wool blankets that had been pulled from the linen closet, to create a makeshift bed, just for the occasion. They laughed. They giggled. They talked shop, as nurses most often do. There were certainly few lapses in conversation as they made up for the time that they had been apart. Of course, Mom told her about the frightening experience on the train. How terrified she had been and how she was having a difficult time adjusting to her new surroundings. She confessed that she was terribly homesick, wanting to go home to her mother and sister. This was particularly true in light of her newly acquired status as mother of a difficult offspring.

The ride back to Norman, on the evening train, was how it should have been. My father met us at the station and was happy to have his little family home. He had heard that there had been a tornado earlier but had no idea that we had been in the midst of it. As Mom clung close to Dad in the front seat, she filled him in on the details of our harrowing encounter with the tornado. Presenting the figurative stiff upper lip had been indeed an attempt in futility. Both of her lips were trembling as she recounted our ordeal. This was followed by a long, uncomfortable silence. It was as if my father had a premonition of what was to come.

Dad knew that his new wife had been desperately homesick for her family. After all, she came from a small close-knit Irish clan and had never been away. Now, more than ever, she needed her mother and older sister to help her with what she saw as the unsurmountable task of taking care of her baby.

Not long after the light on their bed stand had been switched off, and darkness had made everything seem very private, there were whispers that replaced the gentle sounds of sleep. Whispers that, at times sounded quite urgent, sometimes cajoling and casual. But most often, the whispers had a sense of determination, resolution, and calm. The faint chitter-chatter of conversation scurried under their door like tiny white mice in search of a precious chunk of cheddar. First Mom and then Dad, then Dad and then Mom. Voices that indicated that something important was being negotiated.

In the morning, it had been decided. My mother and I would fly to Elmira and stay with my grandparents until the war was over. They were hoping that would be soon. Dad had heard rumblings that President Truman and his war cabinet had been circling the wagons. Hitler was soon to be on the ropes and the Japanese had to be dealt with.

Or so, that was their hope.

Chapter Three
Fasten Your Seat Belt—as told to me by my mother

On the fateful day of our departure, there was a sense of excitement and concurrent dread at the prospect of our leaving. Thankfully, the chaos of packing tempered the pain of my parent's eminent separation as they frantically tried to jam everything into two, soon to be bulging, pieces of baby blue Samsonite. When the suitcases could hold no more, they were placed conspicuously by the front door, waiting for Dad to load them into the back of the station wagon. Mom had to carry me, my diaper bag, her purse, her baby blue makeup case and the mandatory round matching hat bag (a stylish accessory of the day).

Flying, at the time, was a dress up affair. Stockings, high heels and white gloves were an absolute must. Her chestnut colored hair was coiffed meticulously in a stylish page boy and sultry ruby red lipstick made her look like a movie star. Mom dressed me in something pink and ruffled. Add an organdy bonnet, the color of cotton candy with a big brim, a matching knitted sweater with pearly buttons and I was ready to go.

The airport was already a very busy place. It was bustling with military and civilians alike. Soldiers were recognizable in their distinct uniforms. Sailors wore their crisp summer whites and Air Force in cool summer blues. Without question, my father was the most handsome of all in his bell-bottomed whites, his cap perched precariously on his head.

We were departing from gate 47 that was, most naturally, at the far end of the terminal. Mother carried me, her purse and the baby baggage. Dad juggled everything else. Fortunately, he was able to board the plane with us and get us all settled into a window seat situated over the massive wing of the airplane. He lingered as long as he could, making excuses for doing so, until the stewardess indicated that the dreaded moment of separation had come. A quick kiss and he was gone.

Mom stared straight ahead, her eyes wide open, trying to keep the tears where they needed to be. But at last, like water dripping from a leaky faucet, a torrent of wetness poured over the edge. At first, welling up inside her red framed glasses and when they could hold no more, rolled down her cheeks and landed safely in a hankie that she had pulled from her purse.

Mother quickly shoved all our stuff that was not stowed in the overhead bin, under the seat in front of us. Luckily, there was an empty seat right next to her where she plopped me with a bottle full of apple juice and my favorite stuffed bunny, Peter Cottontail. She fastened her seat belt and wiggled in her seat to get comfortable. Certainly, there was nothing to be concerned about. Hundreds of people flew in airplanes every single day and they got to their destination without a hitch. She tucked her purse in the space between her hip and the arm rest, did a quick diaper check and when all seemed quite fine, she took a very deep breath and gave herself permission to sit back and relax.

Slowly the giant silver bird awakened from its slumber, moaning and groaning as the engines began to crank into action. The propellers, one at a time, began to spin. Together they created a cacophony of whirling noises that sounded almost musical. The engines roared "We're ready to go!" And go we did. Thousands of pounds of metal, luggage and human cargo were at twelve thousand feet and heading north east.

Soon the pinging sound and red flashing light indicated to all that it was time to light up. Mom rummaged through her brown leather bag until she finally scavenged a pack of Lucky Strikes and a book of matches. She couldn't help but notice that the matches were from a fancy Italian restaurant that Dad had taken her to for her birthday. The memories of that night encompassed her head like the smoke ring from her lit cigarette. At last, she could finally relax and enjoy her indulgence as she lost herself in thoughts of her husband.

Dreaming dreams of what life had in store for her and her young family when the war was finally over.

Chapter Four
Baby Meets Family—as told to me by my mother

When our plane finally landed at the Elmira airport, Mother was both relieved and excited. As we taxied to a screeching stop on the assigned tarmac in front of gate 7, Mom held me up to the tiny porthole window. She had spotted her waiting entourage behind a huge panel of plate glass and couldn't wait for me to get my first glimpse of them.

Waiting for our arrival were my grandparents and my mother's older sister. It was a small family by anyone's standards, but especially small considering that we were of Irish lineage. The realization that the Irish were famous for large broods of children, made this even more an enigma. Mother didn't have any aunts or uncles in attendance because both of her parents were only children. Likewise, there were no raucous, unruly little cousins with their faces pressed against the glass, waiting breathlessly to meet their new cousin. My aunt was not yet married and childless. So, there they were. My extended family of three.

After juggling our way off the plane and down the lighted tarmac, we were almost home. There was a palpable difference in my mom's mood as she caught a glimpse of her awaiting entourage. It was as if she had morphed, from independent woman, wife, nurse, new mother, back into the security and comfort of her family.

The trio had been huddled together like the varsity football squad in anticipation of not only having the younger daughter back home but also, welcoming a new offspring into the fold. Let's face it, a baby was a big deal. They were few and far between in this family.

My aunt was the first to rush towards us and snatch me from my mother's arms. Mom handed me over with only the slightest bit of reluctance. Now it was my mother's turn, as she threw herself into her mother's soft, fleshy, warm, welcome home embrace.

Love and Marriage and Baby

Mom and Dad are married in Nannie's garden on Herrick Street. Eleven months later.... and baby makes three.

Dad

Mom　　　　Tante　　　　Nannie　　Pa

It was a hop, skip, and jump and we were pulling up in front of 413 Herrick Street. The front porch light spread a welcoming glow across the tiny front yard. Inside the house, every room leaked thin streams of illumination from lamps of every size and shape. When my grandfather turned the key in the lock and swung the front door open, there was a rush of warmth and smells that beckoned one to come inside. Take your coat off, curl up on the cozy couch, rummage through the icebox for some delicious tidbit. In other words, stay a while, this is your home.

My grandmother had a huge cast iron pot filled with beef stew bubbling on the front of the stove. The dinner plates were loaded with mashed potatoes swimming in a sea of brown gravy with bits of onion and mushrooms. Toss on a pile of peas, pull some warm yeasty Parker House rolls from the oven, and dinner was served. Conversation was brisk that night, after all, there was a lot of catching up to do. Dessert was a warm slice of apple pie with a generous chunk of strong, aged, cheddar cheese. My grandmother called it "rat cheese" for reasons that might ruin one's appetite. My aunt had already taken me into the sitting room for a diaper change and my nighttime bottle of Pet Milk formula. It was then time for a brand spanking new pair of jammies, and I was off to slumber land.

The house was a utilitarian space with little room to spare. It had been built for my grandmother's grandmother in the mid 1800's. It had been passed down through the generations with the stipulation that it would always remain so. Upstairs there were two good sized bedrooms and one bathroom with a claw foot tub barely big enough for an average sized adult. Neither one of my grandparents were average in size, I might add.

I shared my bedroom with the two sisters, occupying a corner of the room in front of the bay windows. It was the perfect little nook for the hand-me-down crib that had been pulled, all dusty, from the attic. After a fresh coat of white paint, a made-to-order baby mattress covered with pink and white ticking, a goose down feather comforter, and baby size pillow edged in rose, pale pink, grosgrain ribbon made it ready for its newest occupant. When Tante, that's what my aunt was called, tucked me into bed that first night, my eyelids drooped with sleepiness. Any fears that I might have had were calmed when I spied Peter Cottontail propped comfortably in the corner.

Trepidations about my unfamiliar surroundings soon vanished into a lovely mist of suspended consciousness.

Chapter Five

Oh Tannenbaum—remembered from photos and conversations

We had been residing on Herrick Street for just a few months when it was announced at the breakfast table that we would be going out to the Weaver farm to cut down our Christmas tree. Pa, that was what my grandfather was called, had the day off from his job as secretary of the local YMCA and Mom wasn't on duty at the Arnot Ogden Hospital until three in the afternoon. With only a few weeks until Christmas, Nannie, my grandmother, was anxious to get everything decorated. This was the first Christmas, in a long time, that there was a baby in the house.

A starched, Irish linen, holiday tablecloth, edged with embroidered green and red poinsettias, was pulled out of the bottom drawer of the buffet and after a quick shake, smoothed across the dining room table. Santa and Mrs. Claus salt and pepper shakers took their position as they had for generations past.

I watched as the rest of the family carried boxes and boxes of ornaments, strings of colored lights, bundles of fake garland, Nannie's crèche, nutcrackers, and snow globes upstairs from the basement. Everything was unpacked quickly and placed in their predetermined spot. The placement never, ever deviated from the previous year. The porcelain sleigh took center stage next to the salt and pepper shakers. It was filled with scrunched up silver wrapping paper and blue bulbs were nestled inside like eggs in a robin's nest. Nannie set up the crèche in the front window as she had done ever since her own children were little. Actually, she could never remember Christmas without it as it had been brought to America from Ireland by her grandparents. Irish traditions were the lifeblood of the family.

Inside the house, the garlands were draped over doorways and mistletoe tied with red ribbons dangled from the center. Outside, pine boughs were wrapped around the porch railing like a warm scarf on a cold winter's morning.

It was Pa's job to get the tree in its cast iron tub and twirl strings of lights from the bottom to the top before the ceremonial placing of the angel. When this had been accomplished and my grandmother had made her final inspection, it was all-hands-on-deck to attach the potpourri of glass balls and ornaments. Finally, it was time for the tinsel and there was a time-honored tradition regarding its placement. The silvery icicles had to be meticulously placed, one at a time, over each protruding bough. When the last bit of sparkle was positioned on the final branch of unadorned pine, all lamps were turned off. The lights on the tree were plugged in. As the room was washed with red and green and yellow and blue light, there was a communal gasp of excitement and nods of approval from all the spectators. Now, at last, we were almost ready for Christmas.

Next, it was time for cooking and baking. The importance of food cannot be overstated when preparing for the holidays in this Irish household. But unlike the decorating of the house, Nannie was in total charge of this domain. Food preparation was her bailiwick, and her kitchen was strictly off limits to all other members of the family.

She had learned hard lessons in frugality during the dark days of the Depression and now we were a country at war and many foods had been rationed. In 1942, a food rationing program was initiated and there was a scarcity of many foods. One such food was sugar. Every family was given a "Sugar Buying Card" that was used for its purchase. There was careful planning in everything from the trip to the butcher's shop for the roast of beef, and to the corner grocer for lard, flour, sugar and whatever other basic pantry staples were needed. In the basement, she always had a larder of potatoes, sweet potatoes, and apples heaped high in wooden crates. Mason jars filled with watermelon rind and pickles that had been canned the previous summer made their way up from the cold cavernous cellar.

And then there was dessert. The kitchen was turned into a one-woman pie factory. Apple pie, lemon meringue pie, coconut and banana cream pie, mincemeat and pecan pie. Clouds of sifted flour filled the room like a Saharan dust storm. There was a whirling of ingredients all tossed onto the floured pastry cloth and rolled into perfectly round discs of mouthwatering flakiness. Some pies were topped with fluffy mountains of whipped beaten egg whites. Some were covered with soft blankets of pastry with their tops pierced with the tines of a fork to allow the fragrant fruity steam to escape. Traditionally, the mincemeat had a lattice crust and

Nannie wove the crisscrossing braids of dough with the agility of a Navajo blanket weaver. There was prune whip, tapioca pudding, vanilla custard, lemon curd and chocolate mousse. Finally, there were fruitcakes, bulging with chunks of red and green candied cherries. Each rectangular loaf had been baked weeks ago, meticulously wrapped in white cheesecloth and stored on the back porch, waiting for their daily dowsing of Irish whisky. Finally, there were jelly rolls made with moist buttery sponge cake and filled with raspberry jam and lemon pudding and dusted with a snow like blanket of powdered sugar.

On Christmas morning, the house awakened earlier than normal. Sounds and smells of a very special day floated from room to room. My mother, wrapped in her well-worn royal blue chenille bathrobe, pulled me from my warm cocoon and carried me down the front stairs to the living room, where everyone anxiously awaited my arrival. Brightly wrapped presents with silver and gold curlicue ribbons were stacked neatly under the tree. There was no doubt that Santa Claus had paid a visit to Herrick Street. After all the presents had been opened and mountains of torn tissue paper and discarded boxes littered the floor, it was time for the first meal of the day; Christmas breakfast. We all paraded into the dining room where Nannie had everything ready.

My highchair was tucked between my mother and my grandmother. This placement was not by accident as it was a monumental task to get me to eat. I was old enough to eat mushy table food and considering the fact I never warmed up to jarred baby food and the fact that Nannie was a wonderful cook, should have been incentive enough to coax me into eating. But that was not the case. I was a tiny baby at birth and now, almost a year old, I was still as scrawny as could be. I was not interested in eating, period. No amount of begging, pleading, or playing choo-choo train was going to change my mind. I pushed the food around on my plate hoping that the sheer rearrangement of the scrambled egg would give the appearance that something might have made it into my mouth. Under my toast was a perfect hiding place for the cut-up pieces of baked apple that I was supposed to eat.

Dinner came way too soon, and I was again plopped into my chair, a terrycloth bib tied around my neck. The scrambled egg and toast had been replaced by cooked carrots, cut up into teeny weeny little bite sized pieces and mashed potatoes with gravy. I was still not tempted. Not even when my grandmother tried to bribe me with a promise of a bit of chocolate fudge.

I was not about to fall for that old ploy.

Chapter Six

Baby Takes Three—recounted by Mother, Nannie and Tante

My mother had hoped that when I got over the uncooperative infant stage, life with her baby would get a bit less daunting. After all, there were three very capable women in charge of one baby girl.

Mom was in charge in the morning and early afternoon, until it was time to don her all white nurse's uniform and catch the bus across town to the hospital. She gave me bubble baths in the kitchen sink, dressed me, fed me, changed my diapers and did all those things associated with taking care of the physical needs of her child. After lunch and an afternoon nap, Nannie took over.

Tante was in-charge of my intellectual stimulation and enrichment, so to speak. She took the reins when she came home from her newly acquired teaching position and when Nannie was busy in the kitchen. She was the perfect choice for this assignment as she had just recently graduated from Elmira College summa cum laude and had her Phi Beta Kappa key tucked away in her jewelry box on her dresser. Like my mother, she had, at a very young age, known what she wanted to be when she grew up and had obtained a degree in education to fulfill that dream.

But this was where the similarities with Mother ended. My aunt was serious and rather self-absorbed, with a penchant to overachieve in all things academic and although they were both very smart, she always outshined her younger sister. Over the years, this never spoken about competition had caused a rift between them. Though they had shared a bedroom for their entire lives, they were close in physical proximity only and miles apart in any sort of emotional connection.

Unlike my mother, she preferred the companionship of books rather than people. We spent many hours, just the two of us, sitting in Pa's well-worn recliner with a stack of books that she herself adored. Story after story of Aesop's fables with foxes and crows and low hanging fruit. Volumes by Lewis Carroll and J M Barrie with stories of Alice in Wonderland and Peter Pan. Old leather-bound classics that were authored by Hans Christian Anderson, Robert Lewis Stevenson, poems by Longfellow and English fairy tales by the dozens. I was talked to, read to, and encouraged to parrot verse and rhyme. I was the perfect little pupil, nestled tightly beside her, never moving a muscle, with my eyes glued to every word, every illustration, every flipping of the page. I was like a sponge eager to soak up every last drop of the tales or fables or songs or rhyming verse that were read to me. I was quick to remember all that I heard and held on tightly to every character as if they belonged to me; Gulliver, Robinson Crusoe, Tweetle Dee and Tweetle Dum, and of course, Toto from the Wizard of Oz. I dreamed of living in an exotic faraway kingdom ruled by wicked queens and generous kings.

Being the only child in a house full of adults sparked my imagination to create a fanciful world filled with childlike things to fill my days.

Chapter Seven
A Tragic Beginning—told to me by my Nannie

It was Nannie that took the most care of me from the very beginning and from the very beginning, she was my rock. She was in her own quiet way, the matriarch, the queen of her castle, the one in charge of everything that happened at 413 Herrick Street. It was a tiny domain but none the less, it was hers and she was the chief, cook and bottle washer. This was a position that she relished, and she excelled at. Her training for this position had started at a very young age.

Nannie's family had come to the United States from the coal mines of Ireland in the mid 1800's. The mines of northern Pennsylvania seemed like a perfect fit and had promised them a new life and a fresh start. Like so many immigrants coming from Europe, they shared living quarters with other family members to save money and support each other in their newly adopted country.

My grandmother's young parents were no different. They lived with a spinster aunt and two unmarried uncles. The two brothers went off to work in the mines and Nannie's father had secured a position as a fireman on the railroad. The women stayed at home, maintaining the house, taking care of the men and awaiting the birth of my grandmother. Life in America was not an easy one. There was the harsh unforgiving landscape of the mountainous terrain, weather that was cold to the bone numbing, and dark gloomy skies made even darker and more sinister from the sooty residue of the coal mines.

Every day a well-weathered cauldron of hardy brown stew, with potatoes and root vegetables, took center stage on the wood burning stove and there were golden loaves of bread waiting to be sliced and consumed by the hungry men folk.

On one such day, the ruby red and yellow leaves of September had been replaced by the nearly bare branches of October and Nannie's birth was eminent. Her mother spent her days wrapped in colorful handmade quilts on a makeshift cot in front of the fireplace.

The doctor had suggested that she needed bed rest and because of the cold wind that blew through the cracks of her bedroom window, the kitchen seemed like the ideal place to await the arrival of her child. One particular day, her young husband trudged off to work, as was his usual practice. Bundled against the cold and carrying his black metal lunch bucket filled with warm meat pies, he bid his wife goodbye and headed down the dark rutted road toward the rail yard.

Night came, with little notice of daylight, as winter made its presence known. The miners returned home from their day of hard labor spent underground. Their trousers, jackets, beards, and even their nostrils were filled with the blackness of where they had been. A pot of near scalding water was ready for a makeshift bath, clean clothes, and steaming cups of strong tea would signal the end of their seemingly endless workday. The fragrance of stewed chicken, swimming in a lake of pale broth, was ready to be ladled into earthenware bowls. At any moment, the last of the men folk would be home and the family would be together again. Nannie's mother had the perfect vantage point from her warm bed in front of the fire. She watched, like a cat staring at a bird cage, expecting the latch on the front door to turn and for her husband to be home at last. Her trance was broken when there was an unfamiliar but somehow official, knock on the door. The older brother rushed to answer and with a few mumbled words, closed the door behind him and went outside to finish the conversation. When he returned, he had taken on a ghostly pallor. He was even paler than his Irish birth right intended and his days in darkness afforded. He had taken on a persona reserved only for the most serious occasions, the oldest son, head of the family, had to deliver the news that everyone in the house already knew.

Nannie would be born the following week. Her mother just barely aware of what was going on around her. There had been the typical Irish wake with a steady stream of family and friends. The whiskey flowed and tears were shed but at the end it was just the family. Not the family that they had expected but the family that they were. A young widow, a spinster sister, two bachelor brothers and a baby. My grandmother, my Nannie.

The tragedy that had defined her beginnings, had in no way embittered the life that she had forged for herself. The importance of family was always at the fore. None of her responsibilities were more important to her than the feeding of her tribe. Wonderfully delicious food, prepared as it had been for generations, was what she did, day in and day out, to demonstrate her commitment to her husband, her children, and now her grandchild.

Unfortunately, the newest family member was not at all interested in what she had to offer. Or so it seemed. What she might not have realized was that, although little of what she cooked, baked, fried, or stewed made it into my mouth, she was having a much greater influence on me than the nutritional benefits of her cooking would ever provide.

I suppose the lesson learned was that food not only sustains one's physical being, it also warms the heart, nourishes the brain, and comforts one's soul.

Chapter Eight
My Grandfather, Pa—recounted by family

The holidays were over. The garland was unraveled from the front porch and wrapped like a giant green serpent and placed in its cardboard box to hibernate until next year. Bulbs and bows and all things Christmas were carefully wrapped in old editions of the Elmira Star Gazette and carried back down into the basement. Naked of all its ornaments, the once shimmering Yule tree shivered from the cold, after being tossed to the curb.

There were the short days and the long nights of cold and gloomy winter in Upstate New York. Pa went off to work at the YMCA as he had done for many years. This was a job that he had through the depression when many of his contemporaries were receiving money from the WPA and standing in soup lines.

He was a proud man, a quiet man with few opinions. (It must not be overlooked that he lived in a household dominated by xx chromosomes). He was passionate about little, except for his loyalty to the Brooklyn Dodgers and his disdain for the New York Yankees. He loved everything that had anything to do with baseball. Going to the games, sitting in the bleachers, eating a hot dog smeared with mustard, listening to a game broadcast on the radio or just reading about baseball in the newspaper.

Once, he was photographed while queuing for season tickets at Dodger Stadium and the yellowed picture which had been published in the Elmira Star Gazette hung in a place of honor on the back of the door leading down into the cellar.

He cared deeply for his family, although he kept those feelings where a churchgoing Protestant comfortably kept them. A devoted husband always showed his commitment by being the bread winner and going off to work each and every day. This was exactly what he did.

Every morning, Monday through Friday, he would leave the house while it was still dark outside and walk many miles to his work place in an old stone Federalist building on Pennsylvania Ave. Around four o'clock, he came home for dinner and a quick snooze before walking back to the Y for his evening shift from six until nine. And if there was a basketball game going on, it would be even later. For this, all he asked was that dinner be on the table at five o'clock.

Exactly five o'clock. I'm reminded, that my grandfather was not about to go hungry. He really didn't need dinner at five, as Nannie kept him very well fed. A diet of red meat, mashed, boiled, baked, or scalloped potatoes, all with copious amounts of butter and gravy, nourished a generous ring that circled his midsection.

He was always clean shaven, wire rimmed spectacles sat on his pudgy nose. Suspenders held up his wool tweed trousers and he always wore a heavily starched white dress shirt and conservative striped tie. And the omnipresent hat. Summer or winter, rain or shine or flurries, he always wore a hat. A hat that was not only stylish but covered his conspicuously bald head. Of course, there were brown or black wing tips that he polished every morning. Sensible shoes for walking but still businesslike and professional.

On a rare occasion, I would catch a glimpse of him getting ready for work in the morning. He stood at the bathroom sink in his union suit, a strange one-piece cotton underwear that buttoned up the front. He had a ritual of, each day after shaving, getting a small eye glass out of the medicine cabinet, filling it with warm water and rinsing out his sleep filled eyes. This was followed by a clean shave with a bristle brush, soap and a straight razor. Regardless of his size, he always looked dapper when he headed out the door.

My grandfather saw the importance of education. He was a man who had attended a business college at a time when higher education was certainly notthe norm. For him, a college degree was his ticket to success that brought him status in the community, a paycheck every week and security for his family.

My grandfather was an uncomplicated man...a good man.

Chapter Nine

Bad News—as recounted to me by my mother and grandmother

Pa was seldom included in the daily trials and tribulations of the household. It was surprising that he was huddled with his wife and daughter at the dining room table, after breakfast, one Saturday morning. Tears streamed down Mother's cheeks and Nannie wore a mask of motherly concern with a trace of disapproval in what she was hearing. My grandfather sat stone faced and when all was said, without a word, he pushed himself away from the table and escaped to the sanctuary of his easy chair.

My mother had always been a daughter who had done the right thing, respectful and eager to please. A kid that came right home from school and helped her mother clean the house or pull weeds in the garden or sweep the sidewalk in front of the house. She was pragmatic and down to earth. At a very young age, she knew that when she grew up, she would become a nurse, get married, and have children.

As planned, she had graduated from nurse's training, married her high school sweetheart, and had her first child. All went well until she became a mother. Even with the support of her family, she struggled with being away from her husband. Even more frightening, was the sad realization that something was missing. When she held her child, she had not felt the maternal connection that she had expected. She felt an overwhelming sense of responsibility and she wanted to get away. She just wanted to be with her husband, and she thought it would be best if she left me in the care of my grandparents. So begrudgingly, Nannie agreed. My mother would return to Oklahoma, with the promise that she would travel back home every few months. Mother would leave and my grandmother would take care of me.

It was decided.

Chapter Ten

The Months Go By—as told to me by my grandmother

Nannie and I spent our days happily together. When the daffodils finally poked their yellow heads through the crust of snow and ice, we knew that the end of winter and the fresh beginnings of spring were near. Soon the days were warm enough that Nannie could bundle me up and push me around the neighborhood in my navy blue and forest green plaid carriage. The carriage had been a Christmas present from my two great aunts on my father's side of the family. I was almost eighteen months old now but because I was such a scrawny little thing, I fit quite comfortably in a conveyance meant for a much younger child.

My mornings were spent sitting on the kitchen counter watching my grandmother work her magic. In the afternoon, the two of us strolled around the neighborhood taking in the sights. Nothing terribly exciting ever happened on Herrick Street. There were neighbors out on their porches, and we would linger for a while so that Nannie could catch up on the latest gossip. You know, the usual who died, who got married, who, heaven forbid, might be pregnant.

Nannie shared this story with me after one such visit. In those days, when a woman menstruated, it was commonly referred to as the "curse". A name befitting a woman's monthly cycle. There were no feminine hygiene products yet available so she would have to use wadded up rags in their stead. Rags that she purchased from the rag man's cart as he hawked his wares up and down the streets each day. And even more scandalous, if a woman found herself "with child" and without a husband, she would methodically hang out her freshly laundered monthly assortment of menstrual rags on laundry day, to dispel any rumors of impropriety. This was something that I would understand when I got much older.

When long lit summer days evaporated into longer cooler nights and the leaves on the trees took on hues that were reserved for a particular season, our excursions out into the neighborhood became shorter and shorter. The elms and oaks took on apparitional images as Halloween grew near.

At night the wind howled down our street, shaking giant tree limbs like Mother Nature's skeletons in a horror movie, in preparation for the big night. There were ghosts and goblins, fairy queens and sword wielding pirates, cowboys with six shooters, Indians smeared with war paint, and clowns and witches and zombies.

On Halloween night, as soon as darkness took over the street, the sounds of children's pitter-patter seemed to stream from every doorway. Like a scourge of locusts, they covered the sidewalk in search of the perfect candy treat.

The crowd rushed down the street and made a beeline onto Nannie's front porch. They pushed and shoved, their grubby little hands and frayed old pillowcases outstretched with a chorus of "Trick or Treat". It was not by accident, that throngs of little hooligans found their way to my grandmother's stoop. She was all but legendary, in the neighborhood, for her popcorn balls. Popcorn balls that were so delicious that they were on everybody's "got to have" list.

She had spent the morning popping corn and mixing up a concoction of Karo syrup, butter and chopped nuts that were rolled into perfectly round balls. Finally, each was wrapped in clear cellophane, their ends twisted and tied with orange and brown yarn. In case she ran out, there was an enormous wooden salad bowl filled with Tootsie Rolls and suckers.

Along the railing on the front porch, rows of jack-o-lanterns stood guard, their candles flickering with every gust of cold autumn wind. By nine o'clock the street was empty, and all the little goblins had eaten their fill of sugary confections. There were hands and faces to wash, teeth to scrub, pajamas to jump into and then into bed to continue their Halloween capers in dream land. Indeed, popcorn balls, bubble gum, orange and grape suckers all danced in their heads.

Thanksgiving became Christmas which became Easter. Seasons blew in and crept out almost unnoticed, days became weeks and weeks became months. Mother had managed to get back to Herrick Street, on several occasions, to stay connected with her toddling albeit, still challenging young daughter. She would also provide some well-deserved relief for her mother, who was beginning to show some signs of wear and tear from taking care of a child on a full-time extended basis. Nannie, though she loved spending time with her only grandchild, was looking forward to my parents return.

Chapter Eleven

Good News—as told to me by Nannie and Mom

Finally, the long-awaited news that we had all hoped for. My parents were coming home. Dad and Mom packed up the old station wagon and headed east and then north with an unfettered sense of anticipation and the sudden realization that they were about to embark on a new venture of childrearing and family.

On the day of their arrival, Nannie herded all of us out onto the front porch, where we sat like stony statues on the wooden steps leading to the sidewalk. All eyes were fixed, unblinkingly, on the corner of Herrick and Mount Zoar Streets. There was a subtle shifting of positions only when an occasional car was spotted coming around the corner. There was little conversation, just gasps of excitement at a spotting and then groans of disappointment when it was realized to be just a neighbor who lived down the street.

Without a bit of warning, my aunt bolted from her perch and started running down the street toward an approaching faded yellow station wagon that had just made its appearance. She jumped into the front seat, wildly hugging its inhabitants and after a private moment or two, all three jumped out of the car in front of the house. Mom looked radiant with a smile that covered her entire face but Dad was a vision. Tall, skinny as a rail, with his jet-black hair slicked back, quite handsome and most importantly dressed in civilian clothes.

Our new life was about to begin.

Of course, there had to be a celebratory meal and Nannie had prepared all my father's favorite foods. The seating, at the dining room table, had been adjusted to accommodate his arrival. On this auspicious occasion, my highchair was relegated to the kitchen, as I occupied the seat of honor on his lap. A steaming platter of rosemary scented Swiss steak took center stage with boiled potatoes ready for a dunking in the beefy concoction. Plates were piled high as bowls of buttered carrots, peas, and Brussel sprouts were passed around the table. Any errant gravy was quickly sopped up with slices of Sunbeam bread that had been stacked on a plate ready for just such an assignment. There was the obligatory relish dish overflowing with celery cut into matchsticks, crunchy gherkins, giant pimento stuffed olives, and carrot curls that were held together with colorful toothpicks.

The Sunday china, Candlewick water goblets and the family heirloom sterling silver had been pulled from the cabinet to announce that this was, indeed, a very special night. The Irish linen tablecloth and napkins that Nannie had brought from her mother's house, were meticulously laundered, starched, and ironed before being laid out on the dining room table, just as they had been for special occasions when she was a child.

She wanted to make sure that everything was perfect for her son-in-law's homecoming. Nannie and my father had had a close relationship almost from the beginning. Dad was just fifteen years old when he knocked on the front door wondering if he could walk my mother to school. They dated off and on and at times dated other people but in the end their romance blossomed into something special. Special enough that when Dad got his draft notice, they quickly married in the side garden on Herrick Street with just the immediate family in attendance.

Chapter Twelve

Starting Their Life Together—as shared with me by my mother

The high school sweethearts were about to embark on the adventure of a lifetime. First on the agenda, was to find a cozy little bungalow and set up housekeeping. Mother kept insisting on a three-bedroom house and a big backyard. Why on earth would we possibly need such a big place? There needed to be a bedroom for Mom and Dad and a bedroom for me. Or so I thought. I guess my parents had something planned that I was not privy to. After some searching, they found the perfect house on Spruce Street not far from Nannie's.

Six months, almost to the day, after moving into our new house, my life was about to take an interesting twist. Of course, my Mom and Dad had had the "Wouldn't it be nice to have a baby brother or sister?" talk with me. I guess that this had been a rhetorical question with little relevance to feedback from their daughter. It was quite apparent that they were under the mistaken impression that I was too young to care one way or another. This wouldn't be the first time that they underestimated their first born. But it was way too late for "No thanks, I'm good just the way things are." So, I shook my moppy head in agreement and tried to accept the inevitable. The inevitable happened much sooner than I had expected.

She was pudgy and pink with a perfectly round head covered with the softest of peach fuzz. Her big as saucers, azure, blue eyes sparkled and she cooed with delight at the slightest provocation. She was perfect.

And she ate. She ate with abandon. As soon as her giant terry cloth bib was slung around her neck, her mouth opened like a baby robin and the feeding frenzy began. Spoons full of mushy stuff, that had absolutely no semblance of their past life, went into her mouth. Whatever food didn't make it into her mouth, she wore on her face like a badge of accomplishment. My mother was in heaven.

Mother had a child that ate.

Chapter Thirteen

Time Spent on The Front Porch—from my recollection

Dad had taken an insurance course at a nearby business school, compliments of the G I bill, and had secured a job at one of Elmira's largest and most prestigious insurance firms.

Mom was no longer working, as she had a full-time job taking care of her brood. Every day, weather permitting, my mother would load her two children into the carriage and jiggle over to Herrick Street.

On sunny days, we would swing on the squeaky olive-green glider or curl up on Nannie's lap in the wicker rocking chair. The same rocker that her grandmother sat in to rock her when she was a tyke. On her warm soft lap was where I felt most comfortable. I would breathe in her smells of all-purpose flour and talcum powder mixed with the slightest musky odor of being a woman. She was the epitome of what a grandmother should look and feel and smell like. She was soft and plump with plenty of creases to wriggle into. When I was wrapped in her arms, I felt powerful and important and at the same time vulnerable and needy, knowing that she would protect me from whatever lurked beyond the front porch.

The grown-ups shared hot mugs of strong Irish tea and my sister and I nibbled on sugar cookies. Our perch on the swing was a perfect vantage point to watch the ensuing parade of wildlife. Fat gray squirrels raced around the century's old elm tree by the curb, like Formula One drivers trying to lap each other at Le Mans. Enormous midnight black crows pecked furiously at the ground searching for the overlooked acorn or chestnut. On occasion, there was a foolish, errant dog out for its morning potty run. That was not about to happen in Nannie's yard. She had a rusty old Chase and Sanborn coffee can filled with rocks, on the railing, ready to change any dog's mind. I never actually saw her hurl anything at an animal who dared cross into her DMZ but knowing my grandmother, it was not out of the question.

If we took our positions early enough, we were able to see the Byrne Dairy wagon being tugged down the street, behind a team of shaggy brown horses, on its morning delivery. A perky lad, dressed in a freshly starched uniform, commandeered the wagon. At each house, he leapt from his seat, with milk filled glass bottles rattling with anticipation, and rushed to the awaiting milk box by the front door. The horses, with oversized blinders, stood obediently, with just an occasional flick of a tail, waiting to be nudged along on their journey.

When Mother signaled that it was time to leave, there was always the inevitable fuss. I never was ready to leave Nannie's house. Without a moment's hesitation, I went into refusal mode. Digging in my heels, whining, begging, trying to convince my mother, that she would have time to take care of my baby sister, quality time, time to relax, take a nap. I gave it my best shot. I pleaded with my grandmother that I would be on my best behavior. I would not cause any trouble and as a last-ditch effort, I would be so quiet that she might not even know that I was there.

Chapter Fourteen

Riding on The Bus—remembered by me as recounted by Nannie

Every Friday, Nannie and I walked around the corner and hopped on the Water Street bus for an afternoon of shopping. My grandmother was something of a clotheshorse, tweedy wool two-piece suits in all the fall colors, matching leather pumps with sensible heels, and hats. She was wild for hats. Pill box and cloches, with velvet bands adorned with flowers or feathers depending on the season, were her favorites. For special occasions, there were whimsical veils that floated just over her cheeks.

After a twenty-minute ride on the bus, we were dropped off on the south side of the Water Street Bridge. All that remained was a short but by far the most daunting leg of our journey. Hand in hand, we hiked over the old metal bridge that connected the south side of Elmira with downtown. There was a narrow sidewalk clinging to a span of metal, mere inches from the constant stream of sputtering automobiles venturing across the bridge. When I dared to sneak a peek over the edge, I was terrified by what I saw. I would have a knee knocking glimpse, through the iron gridding, of the roaring Chemung River below. When cars rumbled across, the whole structure shook with a deafening high-pitched whirr of rubber on metal. My pace quickened as I tugged at my grandmother's hand to try to hasten our crossing. At its crest, the bustling city loomed in the foreground. It was literally downhill from there. I stared straight ahead like the horse on the milk truck, blinders in place, until at the bottom, I loosened the death grip on my grandmother's arm.

Once on the other side, all was well. Our route was never changing. There was a time-honored ritual to it all. There was Iszards and Sheehans for everyday items; sheets, towels and such. If a special outfit was in the bargaining, it was the dress department at the Gorton Coy. As we sprinted from store to store, Nannie was like a blood hound, nose to the ground, searching for the bargain basement price that made it all happen.

If I was cooperative, minded my manners, and didn't ask when we were going home, I knew there would be a sugar laden reward at the end of all this frenzy. On the way to the stores, we went right by two of my favorite shops. The Fanny Farmer candy store and a tiny shop that sold boxes of the most mouthwatering caramel corn that was popped fresh every day. Its tantalizing sweet aroma beckoned all that passed by. Stepping inside the Fannie Farmer candy store was like entering lollipop heaven. Suckers of all flavors sat inside the sparkling glass display case... lemon, lime, cherry, grape, orange, root beer.

I was grinning and licking with anticipation as we headed back over the bridge and home. Brown bags filled with stuff draped every inch of Nannie's forearm. Having to lug all of her purchases home was a small price to pay at the end of a successful shopping trip. Veni, Vidi, Vici. She came. She saw. She bought. She carried her spoils of battle back to Herrick Street.

Already a crowd had gathered at the popular bus stop. There were maybe a dozen people already waiting and even more scurried down the sidewalk when the bus was spotted making the turn. As it pulled up to the curb, there was a rush toward the open door as everyone started jockeying for position. My grandmother and I were caught up in the frenzy, sandwiched between the people in the front of the line and the approaching herd. All of that pushing and shoving caused me to come unglued. I was drowning in a sea of brown wooly overcoats, trampled by the throngs of mud encrusted galoshes. I couldn't breathe. I was literally squished like a tomato in a BLT. Smothered by total strangers who I didn't even know. My world was dark, total solar eclipse dark, middle of the night dark. So dark that I was not able to distinguish which coat belonged to Nannie. And her hand, I had lost hold of her hand. I screamed, I screamed at the top of my lungs, I screamed bloody murder. To my amazement, and to the bus driver's amazement, everyone stopped in their tracks. Everyone stared down at the pint-sized little female with her hands on her hips. Without the slightest hesitation, I scolded the offending adults and let them know that I did not appreciate being treated in such a shameful way. By now, my grandmother had scooped me up and deposited me in the seat directly behind the driver. She slipped into the seat beside me, pulled me close and whispered in my ear, "That's my girl."

The love affair with my grandmother continued to evolve...

Chapter Fifteen

That Newfangled Invention: The Radio—from my memories

I was happiest when we were all together. Mom and Dad, my baby sister, Pa and Tante and of course, Nannie. I was especially close to my grandmother. She was perfect in every way. When we were together, she encouraged me to be self-confident and independent. She supported me in the most subtle ways and at a very young age, I felt as if I carried her strength and resolve with me when we were apart.

She was a churchgoing woman, uncomplicated, and God-fearing. She was sheltered and unsophisticated. From her perspective, things were black or white with very little gray. Children were to be seen and not heard. You needed to be kind and honest and clean. After all, cleanliness was next to Godliness. She was not well read, volumes of Proust or Chaucer or Steinbeck or Mark Twain didn't occupy a place on her bedside table. She was, however, a huge fan of Readers Digest, that she read from cover to cover and magazines like Woman's Day and Ladies Home Journal, where if a recipe caught her eye, she quickly snipped it out, and added it to her collection.

At night, after the remnants of dinner were stowed away in the icebox on the back porch, the dishes were drip drying on the drain board, and the meat loaf pan had been declared a "soaker", we all adjourned to the sitting room right off the dining room to listen to our favorite radio programs. The large wooden box that housed the radio was poised in the corner waiting for everyone to get in their designated listening positions. And there were rules. Women and children were not allowed to touch the radio. Pa, the man in the house, turned the ivory colored on/off dial to the on position and that's when the magic happened. Rows of tubes in the back of the box lighted up like a battalion of marching robots in a science fiction thriller. When he searched for a station, if the volume was turned up too high, there was an ear-piercing crackling, or an annoying buzzing, or a combination of both. The twisting and turning of dials continued until he found the program that he was searching for.

Ah, at last, the familiar voices of our favorites. There was Amos 'n' Andy, Arthur Godfrey's Talent Scouts, Burns and Allen, Charlie Chan, Fibber Magee and Mollie, Our Miss Brooks, The Life of Riley, and my personal favorite, the Lone Ranger. It had been one sure way to guarantee some peace and quiet as I sat mesmerized in front of the magical talking box. I was wild about any show that had to do with cowboys and the Wild West.

Give me a six shooter over some silly girlie thing any day. I sat Indian style on the floor, my Dale Evans cowgirl hat perched precariously on my head, wrapped in a raw hide fringed vest and cowboy boots.

Santa Claus had gotten me the cowboy boots the previous Christmas and they were beauties. White leather with brown tassels and silver metal studs that swirled from top to bottom. And guns, two incredibly shiny guns to be exact, ready for a quick draw from my holster with more leather fringe. Cowgirl outfits had lots and lots of fringe. The entire ensemble was topped off with a red and black checkered shirt and matching bandana tied around my spindly little neck. I was a sight to behold.

Christmas...was always my favorite holiday. I loved the tree and the food and the presents. Nothing was more exciting than waking up Christmas morning and tearing through a mountain of gifts. It became even more exciting when my stash included new cowboy regalia. New boots, new gun and holster, new cowboy hat. What could possibly be better than this?

I sat in an almost catatonic state, totally absorbed in what I was listening to. Transported to another time where I lived among my heroes. We galloped on the backs of our mighty steeds, guns blazing, a gazillion hoofs kicking up prairie dust in pursuit of the bad guys. Roy Rogers, Dale Evans, Gabby Hayes and Roy's horse Trigger, The Cisco Kid and his sidekick Poncho, Gene Autry and his horse Champion and of course, The Lone Ranger and his Indian companion Tonto.

"Hi Ho Silver, away".

Chapter Sixteen

Life Before the Supermarket—from my recollections and Nannie's stories

Just after sunrise, the quiet of Herrick Street was broken by the sounds of the ice man's wagon rumbling down the street. Every morning the clip-clopping of his team of horses beckoned me to the curb. This was especially true, on warm summer days, when I flew out the front door to greet him, hoping and praying that he would chip off a sliver of frozen deliciousness for me. I knew that as soon as I had a chunk in my hand and started to slurp, my whole body would be instantly cool.

There was a burlap flap on the back of the wagon. I watched him flip it up, jump up on the platform, and with ice pick in hand, chip off a giant shard of ice. It was huge and cold and crystal clear. With just a few powerful but seemingly effortless jabs, the ice man had a perfectly sized piece for Nannie's ice box. Then with tongs in hand, he threw it over his shoulder and headed toward the back porch.

Daily deliveries of bakery goods also made their way down the street each morning. Nannie would corral the bread man curbside to grab a squishy soft loaf of white bread or a bag of sesame sprinkled hamburger rolls. On special occasions, with a generous amount of begging and pleading, she would buy a package of cinnamon rolls, a yeasty bit of twisted spicy dough hiding under a smattering of white vanilla frosting. Finger licking delicious!

There was also the knife sharpening man who pulled a small cart with a large round grinding stone. If a knife needed sharpening, he would whirl the wheel around by furiously pumping the foot petal and as the wheel turned faster and faster, he held the dull knife blade to the stone and sparks would fly like a handful of sparklers on the Fourth of July.

For all other groceries, we made the trip to Karam's Market, just a short walk down Herrick Street, left on Mount Zoar Avenue and there it was. When the heavy oak and beveled glass door was pushed open, an all too familiar brass bell announced that a customer needed waiting on and Sammie Karam, the owner of the store, was at their service.

It was a small but compact shop making use of every bit of shelf space. Boxes on top of boxes of dry goods, cans stacked on top of cans of soups and vegetables, fruits and juices. All of this somehow resembled the famous leaning tower and every nook and cranny overflowed with bushel baskets of the freshest fruits and vegetables. There was an aisle of bakery items with giant loaves of raisin bread, rolls, and Thomas' English muffins.

In the back of the store, there was an enormous glass fronted display case that highlighted the best reason of all to shop there. Blue white lights gave the huge hunks of stew meat a purplish glow and the chickens looked terribly naked as they squatted in a perfect row across the front of the case. If I stood on tippy toes, I could just barely check out the piles and piles of cold cuts. There was German bologna, cold boiled ham, hard and soft salami and matching cheeses. Nannie loved the liverwurst that she smeared on rye bread with a huge slice of red onion and the stinkiest cheese that I had ever smelled. I had no idea why anyone would eat something that had obviously gone bad weeks ago but if she was enjoying herself, I was okay.

Truthfully, the only reason that I liked going to Karam's at all, was the candy counter in the front of the store. The glass case seemed like a mile long as I stood at the cash register while my grandmother waited for the cashier to bag up the groceries. I pressed my face up against it in hopes that I might be able to morph my way in between the rows of red and black licorice and the sugary jelly watermelon slices. I felt the red-hot atomic fireballs exploding in my mouth and pictured myself biting off the top of a grape filled wax bottle cap and quickly sucking up the purple syrup.

It was the moment of truth. Was Nannie going to reward me for my good behavior? Had I been a good girl? Was she going to have money left over from shopping? Did I really deserve a treat? In a flash, I tried to remember how the day had progressed, but in the end, I looked up at her as she was getting her change and with my most angelic smile begged the question. When a shiny nickel was placed in my hand, I tried to contain my excitement. I had to make it quick as I knew she wanted to get her groceries home and in the icebox. Being always optimistic, I had eyeballed the perfect roll of Necco Wafers (it had the most chocolate ones) and a package of pinwheel caramels with a fluffy coconut filling. Mission accomplished. It was indeed, a very successful shopping trip.

We were home in a jiffy and Nannie scurried to get the groceries put away and start the preparation for dinner. Pa would be home from working at the YMCA soon and dinner had to be on the table at precisely five o'clock.

When he walked in the door, he put his grey tweed overcoat and hat (remember, he always wore a hat because the only hair he had formed a perfect ring around the circumference of his head) on the hall tree and made a bee line to his recliner to read the newspaper and listen to the radio. Mom and my little sister would arrive shortly and Dad was coming straight from the office. Tante would be late as she was tutoring a student at Elmira College to earn some extra money.

My grandmother was all about catering to the men in the family, my father most of all. She had the butcher pick out his biggest, plumpest, most tender rolled roast of pork for dinner, one of my father's favorites. She unwrapped it from its brown butcher paper like the precious commodity that it was. After a good rubbing of salt and pepper and a shower of vegetable oil, it was plopped into a Corning Ware baking dish and tossed in the oven. A head of green cabbage, sliced thinly, was fried with a generous dollop of lard in her well used, cast iron skillet. This accompanied the steamed carrots, mashed potatoes, and no dinner was complete unless everything was bathed in ample amounts of warm brown gravy made from the pork drippings. I was in-charge of the setting of the table. Forks were placed on the left, spoons and knives on the right and fringed teal blue cloth napkins, that matched the tablecloth, were placed under the forks. There were lovely blue flowered dinner plates, salt and pepper shakers, butter dish, and Grandmother Chamberlain's tiny china bowls with gold leaf edges that were perfect for individual servings of apple sauce, always a staple on the dinner table. My father was the last to arrive and when he did, everyone made their way to the dining room table. Nannie was busily transporting steaming platters of pork and potatoes and veggies as her hungry family waited in anticipation. Dinner was a leisure affair of eating and talking and talking and eating. It was a time for the family to relax, recharge and reconnect with each other. On this particular evening, there seemed to be something electric in the air. Something more than just the happenings of the day. Something important that my parents were bursting at the seams to share.

Their news spread like gravy on their plates. Dad's mother, who had been living for some time in Florida, had decided to give him the family homestead in West Elmira. It consisted of a roomy two-story clapboard house built in the late eighteen hundreds and a big red barn in the back with assorted smaller out buildings on roughly five acres. My father, who had always fancied himself a gentleman farmer, was ecstatic and mother imagined having a house with plenty of growing room for her young children. And a garden... there was wonderfully fertile soil and plenty of it for all the corn and string beans and potatoes. And chickens, she had always wanted to raise chickens. It was perfect.

So as soon as all the paperwork was completed, we packed up everything on Spruce Street and moved to Lovell Avenue.

Chapter Seventeen

Moving to The West Side—accounts of my parents and photographs

Sitting on the top of the hill was my father's childhood home that had been given to us by Grandmother H. It sat perched on an oversized parcel of reclaimed farmland with its weathered, gray exterior looking much younger than its one-hundred-year old bones.

There was a well-manicured lawn in front and a row of neatly clipped juniper shrubs stood guard on either side of the front door. Flowerbeds overflowed with the colors of spring and along the driveway there was a line of fruit trees; a plum, a pear, and two apple.

Behind the house, the property took on the appearance of life in the country. Fields of wheat-looking grass stood ready to be mowed and outbuildings dotted the sprawling landscape, awaiting the arrival of someone interested in farming. Most impressive however, was the barn. Of course, it was red and it was massive with two huge sliding doors in the front, that when pushed open, revealed evidence of its past life. Stalls that had housed livestock lined the back wall. Old pitch forks hung like ancient implements of torture that, at any provocation, would leap off the wall in pursuit of an unwelcome visitor. Hidden in the corner was a rusty old John Deere that if it could talk, surely would have answered all the questions of what had been.

Though my dad had grown up here, he had never remembered his father doing any farming. He wasn't terribly handy or outdoorsy or athletic or even remotely interested in planting crops of beans or tomatoes for his family's consumption. My paternal grandfather spent little time at-home and it was no secret that that was the preference of both my grandmother and her husband. He only ventured home on the weekend, spending his work week, on the road, as a salesman for the local can company. Everyone close to them knew that it was not by accident that my father was an only child. Everyone close to them remembered that almost every Friday night, prior to my grandfather's homecoming, Grandma would don her silky, quilted bed jacket and tuck herself into bed with a terrible migraine and a cup of steaming hot tea. Quite convenient and quite telling.

Tragically, his life was cut short when he died suddenly at the age of fifty, two years before my birth. He had gone into the hospital for a routine surgical procedure and had died on the operating table from what was called complications from an incompatible blood transfusion. At the age of twenty-five, my dad was fatherless and for every year thereafter, until he reached the ripe old age of fifty-one, was haunted by the prospect of his own premature demise. This was especially true on the dreaded fiftieth, when I'm sure he blew out the candles on his cake with fingers crossed behind his back.

Now was time for the passing of the proverbial gauntlet. Time for the next generation to take occupancy of the family homestead. A new beginning for the old house. A new husband going off to the office, a new wife busily baking in the kitchen and new children romping on the soft, green grass in the front yard.

Mother and Dad couldn't have been happier in their new digs. There was an abundance of roominess that Mom had not had in their tiny little bungalow on Spruce Street and most certainly, never had growing up on the South Side of Elmira on Herrick Street.

She wasted not a moment putting her personal touches everywhere in the house. There was no ice man in this neighborhood. It was not needed, as a new Amana electric refrigerator purred in a corner of the kitchen. She steamed off the faded wallpaper in the breakfast nook and replaced it with a much more-timely design of dainty little blue (her favorite color) forget-me-nots and a border of dark green paper ivy that crept up the wall. Nannie was really the wallpapering expert and she came every day on the bus to help my mother. After the kitchen, they attacked the ugly gold and gray striped walls of the dining room. Mom chose a wallpaper with a white background and squares of Grecian urns in pale blue and outlined in silver. Quite elegant, quite stylish, and quite formal for a girl from the South Side.

Nannie was a whiz on the sewing machine that took up residence in the upstairs hallway on Herrick Street. A brand-new electric Singer had just displaced an antiquated machine whose power came from the constant pumping of both feet on an iron treadle on the floor. Mother picked out the fabrics, some were thick and nubby with floral brocades to break up the monotony, others were so sheer that you might imagine them blowing in a summer breeze and still others were satin shiny like a debutant's gown. Nannie spun her magic turning a river of sunshine yellow, robin egg blue, ivory and gold, mossy green and pink for her girl's bedrooms into curtains of all shapes and sizes.

It was Dad's Saturday assignment to take hammer to nail until every window was properly dressed. The makeshift furniture that had filled the first house to overflowing seemed lost in the rambling rooms of our new house. But there was plenty of time to hunt for additional dressers for the bedrooms, extra dining room chairs that could be pulled up to the table for holidays and birthday parties and end tables and lamps for the living room and a couple of wing backed chairs for in front of the fireplace and on and on and on.

Nannie scoured the newspaper every weekend for moving sales hoping to find a bargain piece that just needed a little sanding, a coat of fresh paint, and maybe a new bit of upholstery. Mom was a master at painting and Nannie was the wizard of the sewing machine. Every addition of either a piece of furniture or a grouping of paintings or a china cabinet made this house a home. Hand me down heirlooms, thrift shop bric-a-brac, matching salt and pepper shakers and china plates that didn't match at all, made this house a home. Our home. Decorating on a shoestring was not without its trepidations, but my mother and grandmother embraced the challenge and reveled in the final product.

Dad was doing quite well at Perry and Maxie learning the business of auto policies, fire and theft and casualty coverage, deductibles and premiums and all of that insurance jargon. He was, indeed, working his way up the corporate ladder. Money was tight but his professional future seemed promising and my parents felt secure in the fact, that one day, my father would own his own insurance agency. But for now, it was paramount that he work hard, learn his trade, and most importantly make those very important business connections that would pay dividends in the future. Connecting with people was a slam dunk for Dad. He was charming and gregarious, approachable and confident, smart but never tried to impress, fun loving and honest. And if that was not enough for a ticket to success, he was handsome, tall and thin with piercing Paul Newman eyes, a prominent American Indian profile and slicked back hair. You know the old saying about selling ice cubes to the Eskimos. Sales were most likely in his DNA, inherited from his father.

He was going to be successful.

Chapter Eighteen

Tante Comes to Call—as told to me by my mother and aunt

The only drawback of living in the old family homestead was that it was a good thirty-minute bus ride to Nannie's house. Although I saw her most every day, it wasn't the same as being able to walk to Herrick Street for a morning of porch sitting and swinging. And I didn't get to see as much of Tante and Pa.

That being the case, I was more than excited when I saw Tante trudging up the steep incline to our house. My sister and I had been playing cowboys in the front yard when I first noticed her getting off the bus at the bottom of the hill. We scurried into the house to spread the good news but a fresh pot of coffee was already perking on the stove and a plate of chocolate chip cookies sat welcomingly on the kitchen table.

The two sisters spent the next hour or so chatting about stuff that sisters chat about as they munched on cookies and sipped on steaming hot cups of coffee. Mother relished her newly acquired role of woman of the house and for once felt confident that she could, and was, doing something better than her older sister. But any underlying feelings certainly were just that and they actually had a good time relaxing together.

My sister and I were relegated to the front porch with the enticement of a sweet treat and a promise of a reprieve, from our afternoon nap, if we made ourselves scarce. We were more than happy to oblige. After all, these cowgirls

65

had a hankering for chocolate chip cookies. So I was surprised when Mom summoned me to come into the house just as my little sister and I were about to capture some ornery cattle rustlers and throw them into a makeshift jail in the bushes next to the house. That would have to wait.

Once inside, I immediately noticed that on the kitchen table the coffee cups and cookie remnants had been replaced by a stack of official looking papers and sharpened pencils. Tante had taken off her auntie hat and in its stead was Tante, the educator. For some time, there had been some rumblings about how smart I was and how my language skills were far superior to the average four-year-old. Don't all families think that their kid is the smartest child on the face of the earth? Of course they do, and mine was no exception. So Tante plopped me in a chair and administered a battery of tests to prove once and for all, that her niece was above average, smart as a whip, possibly gifted and ready for an early start of her education.

When the test scores were tabulated, my aunt made the long-awaited announcement. As fate would have it, her prediction had been spot-on. She was right on the money...I was off the charts. How could I have ever imagined that this was to prove to be both a blessing and a curse? As one might imagine about expectation and such. And so, it had been decided, I was enrolled in kindergarten at Hendy Avenue Elementary prior to my fifth birthday.

Chapter Nineteen

Off to School—as told to me by my mother and father

On the first day of school, I was yanked out of bed, before the beams of sunlight filtered through my bedroom window, signaling that it was time to rise and shine. My prekindergarten uniform of the day had, most certainly, been my fringed cowboy vest and six shooters. They were nowhere to be found, and in their place, spread out on my chair was a pair of navy-blue knee socks and heaven forbid, A DRESS. The only time that I wore a dress was on Sunday when Mom and Dad took me to Sunday school. Once a week was punishment enough, but now I had to wear one every day? Thank goodness it was not too cutesy or frilly or pink. It was dark blue and forest green plaid with a white collar and skinny green matching belt. Underneath, I wore a white cotton undershirt, white cotton spankie underpants, and a white cotton slip with lace trim that covered the straps and bodice. Tucked just under the chair were my patent leather Mary Janes (usually reserved for birthday parties) that Nannie had gotten for me at the Buster Brown shoe store on one of our shopping excursions. I saw no reason why I wasn't allowed to wear my cowboy boots with the silly dress, but I soon realized that Mother was in no mood to deal with my impulsiveness on this morning. Realizing the futility of my cause, I put on this ridiculous getup, ate a few bites of oatmeal and crawled into the front seat of Dad's station wagon for the quick trip to school. Dad tried to be sympathetic to my plight but explained to me that there was a certain way that well-bred young ladies should look on their first day of school and assured me that I would soon get used to it.

Interestingly enough, Hendy Avenue had been the same school that my father had attended as a young lad. Nothing much had changed. He knew where to park closest to the kindergarten wing and we were lucky to snag the last parking place as cars filled with anxious overwrought parents and their anxious overwrought children jockeyed for position in the battle of the parking lot.

We had received a letter in the mail, several weeks prior, that welcomed me to my first year at Hendy and indicated the room number that I should be brought to, but there was no mention of a teacher's name. When we got to the designated room, I clutched my Dad's hand in a death grip and looked up at him hoping for a sign of affirmation that all would be well. But instead, what I saw was my father's face completely void of all color. Beads of sweat had formed on his furrowed brow. He had taken on a countenance of sheer terror likened to when one sees a ghost. But this was not a ghost, indeed, my teacher's name was Miss Vanderlip and the reason for my father's ashen countenance was that Miss Vanderlip had been his kindergarten teacher many years ago.

It was the perfect opportunity for Dad to turn on the charm, but this woman seemed resistant to anyone who might threaten her dominance. She stood at the front of the classroom, steely-eyed, with her veiny hands poised where, if she had any meat on her bones, her hips would have been. Her diminutive stature certainly didn't lessen the power of her presence. Her hair was just as you would imagine, mostly gray with strands of color from a previous life and it was wrapped tightly in a scrawny little ball plopped at the nape of her neck. My father took a bold step toward the old schoolmarm and with hand extended introduced himself, hoping beyond hope that her memory had aged as much as her appearance. Unfortunately, there was nothing even remotely the matter with Miss V's memory and she let my dad know that my last name on her roster of new students had not gone unnoticed and wondered if it was indeed the next generation that had *returned to the scene.*

Dad smiled a tight little smile and dragged me from my hiding place behind one of his long pant legs. "Good morning, Margaret. Please find your name and sticker in the coat closet and then choose a spot on an empty mat in the circle." Like a murderer being led to the gallows, I grasped at my last opportunity for clemency but instead my father's only comment was that even though my given name was Margaret (an old family name on my mother's side of the family) I had always been called Peg. He then jabbered something about being late for work and blew a quick kiss to his not at all happy daughter who was, by this time, sitting Indian style on her purple plastic mat. I wanted to cry in the worst way but that was not about to happen. There could be no exhibition of girlie emotions. I was, after all, a strong, determined Irish woman. A girl that even in the face of eminent peril had a mind of her own.

I have absolutely no idea why my father had made such an unforgettable impression on his kindergarten teacher. He was never forthcoming with any of the sordid details, but I have a feeling that Miss Vanderlip's apprehension was well-founded and that my father's reputation was well deserved. I was pretty much "a chip off the old block," as they say.

Unfortunately, the first day of school turned out to be an omen of things to come. I'd like to report that Miss Vanderlip's and my auspicious introduction soon morphed into a harmonic, possibly symbiotic, relationship between teacher and child, but that would be an exaggeration at best and most probably a downright lie.

Paramount to the failure of us being able to bond on any level started in the coat closet. This was a rather large space with rows and rows of coat hooks at kindergarten eye level and on the floor was a shelf where boots and rubbers were stored for the day. Just above the coat hooks was a long shelf loaded down with the usual supplies that we would need for our art projects. There were stacks of construction paper organized by color, tins filled with jumbo crayons and skinny yellow pencils, stubby pairs of scissors (so we wouldn't poke anyone's eye out) and huge tubs of white paste, enough to last at least ten years.

Above each hook there was a sticker, a bird sticker to be exact. There were stickers depicting a red breasted robin, a yellow finch with a black head, a blue jay and an oriole, a crimson cardinal, a tiny hummingbird to name just a few. And then there was my sticker. To my horror, Miss Vanderlip had chosen a cow bird sticker to identify my hook. A cow bird...the worst bird in the Audubon bird book. I knew all of this because it was one of my favorite books that Tante read to me. It was an ugly browny blackish-gray crow-like bird that had a reputation for killing the young of the other pretty birds and then laying its eggs in the empty nest. What had I ever done to deserve this kind of humiliation?

There were many, too numerous to mention, issues that I had with this teacher and by the frequency of parent teacher conferences that were held that year, I guess that she must have had a few of her own. There were no concerns pertaining to my academic prowess. I flew through the alphabet, knew all my color words, was on a first grade level for sight words (Tante had made flash cards for me when I was a mere toddler), I could add and subtract, read short stories from my primer, recite my address and count to infinity and beyond. No cognitive inadequacies, no lack of motivation, no falling behind the other students, no developmental delays... as Tante had announced years before "she's off the charts!" Miss Vanderlip's concerns were all about proper behavior or in this case the lack thereof. I talked all the time (I always thought that talking was a good thing). I hated sitting on that cold mat with my toothpick legs all bent inside out like the human pretzel. And with the silly dress on, what if one of those horrible boys could see my spankies? She also thought that my social skills left something to be desired. She told my father, in the most diplomatic teacher verbiage, that I was bossy and overbearing. Talk about the pot calling the kettle black. She was quick to point out that learning to get along with one's peers was crucial to my having a successful year and following directions was a cardinal rule that was not negotiable.

Of course, I promised my parents that I would turn over a new leaf and become the model of civility and decorum in school, remembering Nannie's maxim that little children should be seen and not heard. I had every intention of reining in my enthusiasm. That's why it was such a shock when Miss Vanderlip ordered me to go sit in the coat closet after I accidently tumbled over a stack of blocks and landed in a heap in the middle of Irving Paltovick's medieval castle that he had been toiling over for the last half an hour.

That closet was the last place that I wanted to be, subjected to this kind of isolation where I was forced to look at all those pretty bird stickers on everyone's coat hook but mine. This was torture. This was like prison, kindergarten solitary confinement. There was no place for me to sit so I grabbed some coats and made a cozy little mound to perch upon while I contemplated my fate. A thin stream of light crept through the slightest crack in the door, enough light for me to spot a stack of books that were just within reach. I teetered on tip toes until I was able to grab the edge of one of the books. It was a good plan until the entire stack tumbled off the shelf in an avalanche of words and pictures. There is however, more bad news because along with the books, a giant glass jar of glue joined the fracas and splattered in a kazillion pieces on the floor. There was a loud crash and almost instantaneously Miss Vanderlip appeared at the door, hands on hips and a most unpleasant expression on her face.

Dad came to school and found me in the principal's office.

Chapter Twenty

The Rabbit House—with fond memories

Summer vacation came not a minute too soon. No more pencils, no more books, no more teacher's dirty looks. Alas, I was free. Free to ditch the dresses and put on some real clothes. A plaid flannel shirt, fringed rawhide vest, blue jeans, a cowboy hat, white tasseled western boots and my holsters packed with my six shooters.

During the hot days of summer, we were shooed outside to entertain ourselves in the sprawling unkempt back forty. Mother would say, "Outside girls and get the stink "blow'd" off you."

When my sister and I weren't rounding up the bad guys or playing with our dog Jip or building a fort with discarded cinder blocks and old blankets, we would venture into the wooded corner of the property. There stood a dilapidated, shambles of a house, that had long ago been abandoned, where we could play.

We called it the "rabbit house" because there was always a family of rabbits that lived inside a rusty storage bin in the basement. On the west side of the house there was a rickety wooden porch that led to the front door and just inside the front door was the parlor (or what remained of the parlor) and in the far corner was a piano with its lid opened and like a medical student's cadaver, its parts and pieces had been removed for closer scrutiny.

Sometimes we just sat on the front steps and listened for sounds. I'm not sure what we were listening for, but people had, for years, said that our rabbit house was haunted. Now that being said, we never (well, almost never) heard anything that might give up its secrets. There were no moans or groans of inhospitable ghosts, no doors that slammed shut on a windless afternoon, no creaking floorboards or foreboding chains rattling in the attic.

Mostly we heard the chirping of songbirds as they built their nest on the outstretched arms of the giant maple and oak and chestnut trees that shaded the house. We heard squirrels and chipmunks as they made hunting for acorns look less like work and more like play.

However, there was one rather overcast afternoon when all of that changed. We were sitting on the porch, building "something" with interesting stones and pinecones and other bits of flora that we had been collecting for a while. We were so engrossed in the task at hand, that we were oblivious to the ever so subtle changes that were happening all around us.

The late afternoon sky suddenly seemed more like nighttime, dark and ominous. A particular wind blew across the porch like it was trying to tell us something. The old house creaked with displeasure as if it had been prematurely awakened from its afternoon nap.

And then there was a thud, not just one but a succession of thuds, thud, Thud, Thud, THUD. Whatever the noise was, whoever was making the noise, it was getting closer and closer with every bone chilling terrifying thud. We had just enough time to run for our lives and run we did, screaming like banshees across the field and down the dirt road toward home. When we got far enough away that we no longer feared being gobbled up by some creature from a horror movie, we slowed our pace, took a deep breath and vowed that this would remain our sister secret and was something that would not be shared with Mother.

Chapter Twenty-one

Dad the Builder—from pictures and talks with my father

Life was good in the front house at Lovell Avenue. However, my dad, who fancied himself the gentleman farmer/part time contractor, was now toying with the idea of somehow converting the old red barn behind the house into our new digs. It was decided.

Plans that were, at first, scrawled on scraps of notebook paper and cocktail napkins, morphed into official looking blueprints that were sent to the city for approval.

There were cinder blocks delivered and stacked one on top of the other next to the barn and an endless caravan of lumber yard trucks chugged up our driveway with load after load of building materials.

Money was tight, so my father was doing all the renovation work, whenever he was not at his day job. Every weekend and every night after work he was hammering and sawing and measuring. The old siding had to come off and there were two by eights ready for framing. The piles of cinder blocks slowly disappeared as they were slathered with mortar to shore up the crumbling foundation.

After the framing was completed, there were sheets of plywood to be nailed in place and everything was covered with tar paper. Finally, a wood siding was secured and finished off with a coat of olive drab green paint.

The barn was two stories, so Dad had to set up scaffolding on the perimeter to reach those high places. Did I mention that my father hated, hated, hated high places and was terrified of heights? He would always try to commandeer my mother for the real high jobs as she didn't have height issues and she was also quite handy with a hammer.

The new roof was dried in and dressed with row after row of gray and gritty asphalt shingles. New windows had taken up residence in the gaping holes that were framed in and doors were hung, one on the front of the house and one on the back. The front door was quite fancy with frosty panes of beveled glass. The back door was quite plain. It led to the vegetable garden and Mom's clothesline where snow white bed sheets and shirts and terry cloth towels fluttered like a flock of gulls on laundry day.

With my father at the helm, the renovation progressed. White collar insurance salesman by weekday and blue collar carpenter, plumber, electrician by night.

After the exterior of the house (it could no longer be called a barn) was completed, it was time to begin the work inside. What had once been horse stalls in the back, became a spacious living room with a giant picture window that provided the perfect vista of rolling fields, a row of apple trees, and a towering blue spruce with furry boughs laden with prickly pinecones.

There was a dining room, next to the kitchen, where my mother envisioned family and friends gathering to partake in the most scrumptious Sunday dinners or draped with crepe paper streamers for birthday parties. Of course, there would be holidays when the table would be overflowing with the quintessential roasted turkey, filled with sage scented stuffing or baked ham, studded with aromatic cloves.

Mom was anxious to start creating memories for her young family, much the same way that her mother had created memories for her and her sister. She would continue the tradition of nurturing and the demonstration of a mother's love through the meticulous preparation of meals from recipes that had been passed down through the generations of our Irish roots.

The kitchen was filled with natural light that streamed in through a set of windows over the large double sink. There was an abundance of counter space perfect for rolling out pie crusts. Pine cabinets lined the walls, ideal for storing and stacking. There was open shelving for spices, oft used utensils and all sizes and shapes of bowls. Gone were the days of the ice box and wringer washing machine. Mom had all the most modern appliances; a four burner, state of the art, gas range and an Amana electric refrigerator and freezer. A corner of the kitchen had been reserved for a lovely round mahogany table that Mother had found at a flea market and had restored to the treasure that it had once been. Without a doubt, no home was complete without a place for the family to gather for everyday meals of scrambled eggs and toast, peanut butter and jelly sandwiches and Friday night potluck dinners.

Upstairs, there were three spacious bedrooms, plenty of closet space, and large windows, perfect for keeping out the bone chilling January winds and capturing those all too illusive breezes on hot summer nights. My parents' bedroom extended the entire length of the house (bowling alley comes to mind). Regardless of its extravagant size, Mom and Dad slept in tiny twin beds, ala Ozzie and Harriet, as was the customary sleeping arrangement for many a married couple in the 1950s. Strategically placed around the room was a hodgepodge of hand-me-down furniture. There was a double dresser for Mom's tops, slips, nightgowns and such and a tall chest of drawers for Dad's clothes. A cedar chest for linens and two wicker rocking chairs filled the far corner of the room. There was a large bathroom that the whole family shared at the end of the hall.

By late September, my parents started making a concerted effort to get the dry wall hung and taped, the electrical up and running, water pipes connected, and a furnace installed before winter reared its ugly head. The days were getting noticeably shorter and colder as they pushed to the finish line, hoping that whatever was left to do, could be done with the comfort of heat, lights, and water.

The house remodeling was chugging along at full throttle, until one evening, when there was an unexpected phone call from my Grandmother H who lived in Florida. The good news was that there was not a medical emergency, she was just fine. The bad news was that she was just fine and was coming for a visit. She was driving north to see the fall foliage with all those beautiful colors of gold and orange and crimson. During the call, she had put my father on notice that she would be staying with her son and his family for an extended lay over.

Now, if that wasn't a bit stressful, the very next day, my parents learned that Dad's aunts were also coming for a visit.

Mother wanted everything to be perfect when Aunt Kathleen and Aunt Betty came to call. The house had to be perfect, the lunch had to be perfect and my sister and I had to be perfect. After all, they were driving all the way from Corning, New York to visit and Mom was determined to make a good impression with my father's relatives.

From the moment they stepped in the front door, they gushed with compliments about my mother's decorating prowess, her choice of wall color, wallpaper, the furniture, the drapes and the carpets. Yes, the house was a hit...check one!

Lunch was served in the dining room on the fancy china, cloth napkins spread in our laps and sterling silver in hand. Mother served tuna casserole, hot rolls, iced tea and for dessert, chocolate angel food cake. I was thrilled to be invited to sit at the table with the grownups and I had promised Mom that I would be on my best behavior. Yes, the lunch was a hit...check two!

My sister had been napping during lunch and my aunts were anxious to see her. We paraded upstairs, mother in the lead. She pushed open the door and there was a terrifying gasp, followed by a stench that could only be described as heart stopping and stomach churning. As we pushed forward into the room, it was all too obvious what had transpired. My sister had decided to decorate the wall next to her crib with the most ingenious artwork. I want to say it was modern art using the only medium available...the contents of a long-forgotten diaper.

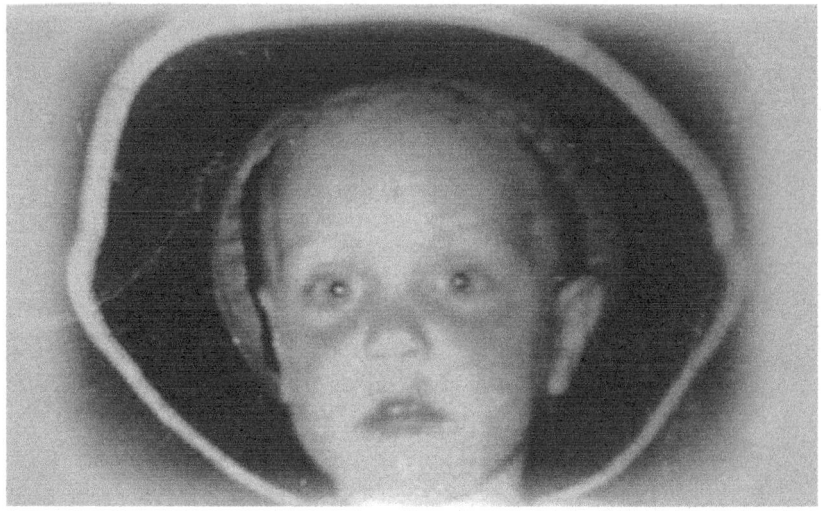

We waved goodbye as my aunt's car sputtered down the hill. There were no words to describe what had just happened.

Chapter Twenty-two

The Other Grandmother Comes to Visit—from my memory

Grandmother Havens arrived from Sarasota with a minimum amount of fanfare. Mother and she had little in common and had never really hit it off, but Mom was anxious to make her stay with us, a pleasant one.

There were groceries to buy, meals to plan and prepare and the house had to sparkle from top to bottom. Bowls of late summer flowers from the yard were strategically placed around the house, on the dining room table, and on the entry table in the hallway. On the nightstand in the guest room, was a crystal vase, brimming with pink rose buds that would welcome her mother-in-law.

Everything was ready when her road-weary, old gray Studebaker pulled up to the curb in front of the house. Mother pushed us out of the front door and with a "please be on your best behavior" steely glare herded us toward the grandmother that was, for all practical purposes, a stranger.

She was nothing like Nannie. She wasn't soft and plump and approachable. She was tall with scarecrow straight posture, stick thin (one might even consider her bony) and her skin was lined and leathery from too many years of lying in the unforgiving tropical sun. And trousers, she wore trousers. I never saw Nannie wearing trousers or any other woman for that matter. Never. She was her own woman, very independent, living alone far away from the family and only making her sojourn north to New York once a year.

Like obedient baby ducklings, we waddled down the driveway staying safely behind Mother and as we approached, our grandmother's face showed only the most superficial signs of interest in embracing the children of her only son.

After a perfunctory peck on the cheek and pat on the head we were instructed to get our gifts from the backseat of her car. I tried my best to act thrilled as I retrieved shoe boxes of seashells. They were beautiful, mind you, all pink and blue and striped and scalloped and a perfect addition to my already extensive collection from last year.

Mom played the "so glad you're here" daughter-in-law as she escorted Grandma into the house. Dad emptied the car of a small, medium, and large suitcase, a bulging plaid garment bag and cardboard boxes all taped and labeled for future disbursement. I assumed that somewhere in this bounty there was a box of shells for Mother, a box of shells for Nannie and boxes of shells for her two sisters who lived in Corning. Everyone in the family would be adding to their shell collection this year. No one would be left out.

I guess with all the excitement, Dad had absentmindedly left the door of the car open and his two young daughters were left curbside. There I was staring into the inside of the abandoned car. How interesting with all the knobs and dials and switches just waiting to be explored. There was a half full box of pop up tissues and a well-traveled road map on the passenger seat. A thread bare beach towel, embossed with a faded pinkish flamingo, was carefully tucked over and around the driver's seat.

I just wanted to take a quick peek inside. After all, I was a curious child and all those knobs were oh so tempting. Every footstep closer to the open door was accompanied by an over my shoulder glance, first at my little sister and then the front door of our house. And yes, my sis was still glued to my shadow behind me and Dad and Mom were still way too busy inside and nowhere to be seen.

Standing on tippy toes, I just managed to pull myself up onto the running board, where I grabbed the rusty metal seat frame and tugged, with all my might, until I was sprawled across the dirty floor of the passenger side. Success, and now I just needed to reach down and grab the outstretched hands of my sister and all would be well. One, two, three and up she came. There was no way that I was going to be able to get her up on the seat, she would have to be content with the view from the floor and she seemed quite happy with right where she was.

I crawled across the seat until I was perfectly positioned behind the steering wheel. Why did it seem so much bigger now than when I was standing on the outside looking in? I got up on my knees so that I could just barely see out of the windshield and positioned my hands on the steering wheel like I had seen my dad do so many times. Motor sounds of vroom, vroom, vroom, came out of my mouth with such a roar that it filled the whole car and the faster I turned the wheel, the louder the roar became. It was beyond my wildest expectations...I really could feel the car moving...I was driving my grandmother's car. Seriously, it really felt like the car was moving.

Reality struck when my parents came catapulting out of the house with arms flailing, their contorted faces a hideous shade of red, and mouths wide open with the expectation that some blood curdling screams were about to pour out. And pour out they did. I don't exactly remember what they were screaming, but I do remember hearing my name, not just once, but many, many times.

Dad tore down the hill, across a neighbor's yard, and jumped into the runaway car, which by now had slowed considerably. He yanked on the hand brake as we came to rest in a ditch by the side of the road, missing by inches, a telephone pole and a stop sign. My father's heroic reaction had ended my adventure and prevented the car's downward plunge toward a major thoroughfare at the bottom of the hill. Tragedy was averted and all ended well.

For the next several days, actually until my Grandmother left, I was exiled to my room. There would have been a time when I would have protested this kind of isolation. I would have pleaded my case that I was being treated unfairly, blamed for something that I didn't even do, misunderstood, but not this time. Indeed, I relished my confinement. I was more than grateful to be spared a scolding, a lecture, or possibly even a spanking.

No, I was perfectly content to hide out for a while until the dust literally and figuratively settled.

Chapter Twenty-three
The Long-Awaited Move—from my recollection

Winter was a blur of dark and gloomy, with Artic winds that would chill anyone adventurous or maybe fool hearty enough to venture outside. Even the sun seemed to have escaped to the warmer climes of the tropics. But Mom and Dad continued to make progress on the back house, as it was referred to, and all seemed ready for us to make the trek from 966 Lovell Avenue to 966 1/2 Lovell Avenue.

One morning when I bolted out the front door late for school, I realized that something had changed. Something seemed different. Something was in the air, something fresh, something just a tad bit warmer clung to a still wintery breeze.

We jumped into the front seat of Dad's new Chevy station wagon (Dad was doing well at Perry and Maxy) and as we sputtered down the driveway my father rolled down his window and proclaimed the obvious, "Spring has sprung!" and the back house was ready for us to take occupancy.

Empty boxes that Dad collected on his way home from work began piling up in the corner of the garage in preparation for the upcoming move. Everyday Mom designated a kitchen cabinet or dresser drawer or closet shelf for packing, hoping to get a jump start on the daunting task at hand. Seldom used pots and pans, white Corning ware, stackable baking dishes, muffin and cupcake tins, roasting pans in small, medium and large, and a mishmash of other hand-me-down utensils, were meticulously wrapped in old newspaper and piled, one on top of the other, in the boxes until every nook and cranny could hold no more. A generous swath of masking tape wrapped the bulging cardboard containers and with fingers crossed were labeled and dragged to the "done" area of the garage. And so the empty boxes, one by one, were filled to overflowing, labeled, taped and stood ready to make the march to their new home.

Our neighbor in the back had agreed to let Dad borrow his truck for the weekend. Bright and early Saturday morning, everyone got roused and ready for the big move. Mother Nature cooperated with plenty of sunshine and there was not a single puff of a rain cloud in the sky.

By Sunday night, we were happily ensconced in the back house. Bed frames were put together, mattresses plopped on top and covered with freshly laundered linen, fluffy goose down pillows, scratchy wool blankets and finally, chenille spreads. Dressers were filled with underwear and socks and shirts and shorts.

My school clothes and party dresses neatly hung in my closet. My cowboy wardrobe made the journey safely and I was relieved when all was accounted for. Mom had put a special set of hooks on the back of my bedroom door to hang my vest and plaid shirts. My cowboy hat fit perfectly on a shelf in my closet and my boots stood tall next to my Mary Janes on the floor.

I had convinced my mother that the perfect placement for my bed was right in front of my bedroom window. I would have the perfect vantage point to spot any errant cattle rustler who might foolishly wander onto my property. It would also provide me with an unobstructed view of our driveway so that I could spot Nannie's little blue jalopy coming for a visit.

Chapter Twenty-four

The Garden—from photos and memories of living off the land

My parents were anxious to get the inside of the house organized so that they could take advantage of the first warm days of spring and get the garden ready for planting. Dad pounded stakes into the rich but rocky soil to identify the boundaries (approximately 80 by 40) and with the Burpee seed catalogue in hand, they created a blueprint of sorts with a long list of must-have vegetables that they wanted to include.

There would be at least three rows of sweet corn, a row each of pole beans, white wax beans, leafy lettuce, peas, carrots, radishes, zucchini and yellow squash, green peppers, scallions, and most certainly beefsteak tomatoes. There would be an abundance of yummy vegetables that would last well into the fall and Nannie and Mom would can much of what was left over to be enjoyed even when the garden had been plowed under and covered with a snowy white coat.

My father rented a tiller to prepare the soil and we trailed behind picking up chunks of rock and anything else that might interfere with the growth of our seedlings. Mother followed and with a hoe, cut a trench into the newly plowed earth just the perfect depth and width for the seeds. Following their plan, the seed packs were torn open and one by one they found their new home. Row after row, after row, until every last seed was in the ground, ready to be covered with soil and given a generous watering.

Every morning, Mother would venture into the garden in hopes of spotting the tiny plant heads as they pushed toward the sun. Thankfully, it was the best spring ever for growing with many warm rainy days in April. May was equally as warm but long sunshine filled days replaced the early spring showers.

By the time school was out in June, the garden had evolved from beautiful brown to glorious green. So many greens...and leaves of all shapes and sizes...and blossoms all shades of yellow and white. The tomato and bean plants were ready to be staked and Dad built an elaborate trellis system to lift the fragile tendrils off the ground. Mom pointed them in the right direction as she gently wrapped them around the base of the trellis.

Many an afternoon, I sat Indian style between the rows of knee-high corn, waiting for their ears to pop out of the stalks and celebrating when every ear had a tassel of golden silk that drooped happily toward the ground. For hours I sat in the presence of my newfound friends and if I stayed statue still, I could almost hear the entire garden exhale precious oxygen that surrounded me as if it had a life of its own. I rummaged through the trails of squash and zucchini vines hoping to find that one of the lovely blossoms had turned into the tiniest of vegetables.

Every day, I would check on their progress and be amazed of how quickly everything was growing. When the tomatoes were a deep reddish purple and hung heavy on the vine, Mom plucked one off, wiped it on her apron, and we took turns chomping off huge warm bites, with juice spurting in all directions and tiny seeds that we slurped with abandon.

Once I realized that the carrots and radishes, unlike the peas and pole beans, grew underground, I couldn't wait to rip them out of their cozy incubator and announce to my mother that they were ready to eat. "Be patient" she lamented, as she tried not to notice the hand full of carrots that I had hidden behind my back.

Mom had reserved the northwest corner of the garden for the planting of potatoes. Like carrots and radishes, they also grew underground but instead of pulling them out by their leafy tops, I had a child size hoe that I used to unearth my buried treasure. When that was too slow, I dropped to all fours and started digging in a canine induced frenzy until Mother Nature's booty was ready to be scrubbed and boiled and buttered for their debut on our dinner table.

There was one vegetable that I was not anxious to harvest and those were the dreaded yellow wax beans. Unfortunately, they were my Dad's favorite. When he was a boy, his mother would boil them up and cover them with a disgusting blob of nondescript grayish béchamel sauce. But even with a healthy dose of salt and pepper, there was no saving them. I did everything humanly possible to gag them down. I tried to bury them in my mashed potatoes, wash them down with an ocean of tap water, or hide them in the bottom of my glass of milk. When all else failed, I stuffed a giant fork full into my mouth and simultaneously plugged my nose and chewed with abandon. Praying the whole time, that the gray, globby mass would find its way to my stomach.

My shenanigans did not go unnoticed. Nothing annoyed my mother more than my refusal to eat whatever was put on my plate. "After all, there were starving children in China," Mother would scold. But most probably she just recalled her parent's struggle to put food on the table during the Great Depression of the 1930's and again during World War II in the forties when many foods were rationed, expensive and hard to come by. Food was never wasted, and food was never taken for granted. Food was celebrated. Food was love.

Mother never forgot that Nannie's culinary skills turned little into luscious or how she morphed a ham bone into a yummy meal of ham flavored baked beans, all deliciously sweet with brown sugar and molasses. She remembered how Nannie's best friend Freddy, who worked in the kitchen of the Elmira Country Club, would smuggle an old beef bone home wrapped in her apron and buried in the bottom of her giant faux leather handbag. The next morning, they marveled at their good fortune as the two friends huddled over the giant bone that they had stashed in the icebox. Lying there before them was all that they needed for a half dozen hardy dinners. All created from a bone that was naked of anything that one might call meat. But it was a beef bone filled with marrow and sinewy strings of grizzle. It alone, would give their stews and gravies the taste and velvety texture of a juicy standing rib roast of cow.

Chapter Twenty-five

Summer Wanes—from memories of long ago

Nannie arrived early one already warm and humid morning and found Mother busy getting the kitchen ready for a marathon canning session. Mason jars and corresponding lids were pulled from corrugated cardboard boxes and were swimming in a giant pot of roiling water. Huge metal tongs, laid next to the pot, waiting to rescue the scalding jars from their bath and a mishmash of dish towels spread out on the countertop were awaiting their arrival. Bars of paraffin wax bubbled into liquid on the front burner to seal the jars of strawberry jam.

It was an assembly line that even Henry Ford would have been envious of. The bushel baskets of perfectly ripe tomatoes were given a scrubbing in the kitchen sink and plopped into a cauldron of boiling water, just long enough for their skins to pop, making them much easier to peel. With arms flailing and knives swirling, the round ruby orbs were sliced and diced and chopped and mashed and pureed into a medley of tomato perfection. All of this was spooned into the awaiting jars.

Finally, each jar was placed in a water bath so that everything cooked into yumminess. There were jars of tomato sauce to be poured over pasta, jars of sliced tomatoes with sprigs of dill weed, jars of tomato chunks waiting for the perfect pot roast and jars of chili sauce all red and green and sweet and tangy.

Nannie filled a box of assorted jars and loaded them into the back of her car for their trip to Herrick Street and their new home in the dark, musty basement. Whatever was left, we carried into the storage room, behind the furnace, where Dad had built some shelves for Mother's canned foods from her garden. Every jar was placed on their spot with thoughtful consideration. Stepping back at intervals, wanting to make everything perfect, she turned each jar just so.

She marveled at what she saw.

Chapter Twenty-six

The Circus Comes to Town—remembering that everything seemed so big

I loved looking out of my bedroom window and imagining from that vantage point, I could see everything. In the morning, I was the first to spot the milkman's truck tootling up the driveway, a faint cloud of exhaust and dust followed it to our milk box on the front porch. No longer was milk delivered by horse and wagon. This was the 1950's for crying out loud. Milk was delivered by gasoline power not by a hay chomping equine.

But I was always most excited when I caught a glimpse of my grandmother's car making the turn off the main road and heading toward our house. Even if I didn't see her car, it was not a problem. I knew exactly what it sounded like. I can't explain it, I just knew.

One morning in the darkness, before there was even a suggestion of morning, way before the sun was up and I was still all snuggled in my bed, I heard her car coming down the driveway. Her headlights were barely visible in the predawn fogginess, but I knew it was her.

This had to be the day that I had been waiting for. The day that Nannie was taking us to the railroad siding, adjacent to the fairgrounds, to watch the Barnum and Bailey circus train come to town. It was scheduled to arrive at five o'clock AM and every kid in town wanted to be there. When we arrived at four thirty, there was already a crowd gathered near the tracks. Nannie dragged my little sister and me through a slight opening between the throngs of exuberant children and the barricades that the circus used to keep the spectators at bay. Public safety was their reasoning, but Nannie saw it as a major annoyance. We finally made our way to the perfect spot for viewing and we huddled close to our grandmother for fear that we would be trampled in the melee.

At last, someone spotted the train in the distance and their excitement spread like wildfire through the anxious crowd. I felt the ground begin to shake where I was standing and then the unmistakable roar of the giant engine came leaping out of the darkness, coming to a screeching halt right in front of me. It was huge and black and noisy. It was so menacing that I burrowed my face deeply into my grandmother's wooly coat. There it was, the train of all trains, the train that carried all the circus animals to their destination.

Nannie gently coaxed me from the safety of her coat and nudged me forward to get a better view. Before I actually could see anything, I could hear the roaring, the blatting, bellowing and the growling. Noises that only something totally wild and wonderfully dangerous could conjure up from their furry diaphragms.

And the smells, smells that whirled around inside my nostrils. A sweet mixture of smells, a potpourri of odors, of diesel fuel and hay and piles of dung that would make you stare in disbelief. It was astonishing that I was both shocked and at the same time somehow perversely fascinated when I encountered such a pile.

Unbridled curiosity had replaced my fear of being eaten alive by a rogue Bengal tiger as I inched closer and closer to the cages. The big cats were right in front of me and there had to be at least ten barred enclosures painted in startling circus colors. The lions paced back and forth as if they were all too aware of the impression that they were making on their young, awestruck audience. Likewise, the majestic white tigers and the sleek angry leopards were all in perpetual motion, back and forth, back and forth.

There were box cars filled with magnificent horses that would soon be prancing around the center ring of the big top. Equines all plumed and sequenced matched their lovely bareback riders. Riders so skillful that they appeared to be affixed to the mighty steeds like brides on a wedding cake.

We felt ourselves being carried further down the railroad siding by the sheer magnitude of the crowd. We soon discovered what all the excitement was about when someone in the front screamed, "The elephants! They're unloading the elephants!" As I strained to catch a glimpse, there they were. In all their gorgeous, humungous splendor. The ground trembled as they were herded by us, their ears flapping, and their trunks obediently hanging on tightly to the tail in front of them.

Everything and everyone moved swiftly away and as quickly as all the animals arrived, they were gone. I would just have to wait until tomorrow, when I would be sitting under the big top, eating great globs of pink sugary cotton candy and buttery popcorn.

My heart racing with excitement for the start of what was advertised and without exaggeration, the "Greatest Show on Earth".

Chapter Twenty-seven

The Cottage on Seneca Lake—remembering chasing lightning bugs

My mother and father had big plans, big ideas, big dreams. They were hardworking, full of expectations and energy... go getters that saw success in their future. These were good times, the 1950's, post-World War II, post-Depression. The country was prosperous and so were my parents. Opportunities were available to them that were unimaginable for the previous generation. The timing was perfect to make the American dream for my parents a reality. There was the big house, albeit the big renovated barn, a fairly new car and enough money to take care of all the necessities and make even some luxuries possible.

One such luxury was membership in the Elmira Country Club. Just two blocks from our house, it was the perfect venue for my parents to socialize and for my father to make those ever so important "business connections". There was golf for Dad and a pool, where my grandmother could drop us off for a day of swimming. There were gin and tonics for the ladies on the patio on warm summer afternoons, dinner and dancing in the main dining room, and an occasional male-only card game in the back of the men's locker room.

It was at one of these poker games that Dad met Mike Landon, a prominent businessman from an old established Elmira family. They had much in common including their passion for the game of golf and a fondness for an occasional rye and soda after eighteen holes. It was during one of these lazy early evenings, while relaxing in the club house, that Mike mentioned that there was a cottage for sale right next to his on one of the nearby Finger Lakes. He was friends with the seller and made arrangements for my parents to take a look at it on the weekend.

Bright and early, on Saturday morning, we all piled into the station wagon and made the hour-long trip north to the village of Watkins Glen. From there, we chugged up the east side of Seneca Lake until we saw the Hector Falls sign. The very next road was the road to the cottage. Mother was a bit reluctant as we turned onto something that would be best described as little more than two dusty tire worn strips separated by tall weeds. This was hardly a road but more like a path, a very windy, bumpy, curvy, rutted, down the side of a steep embankment, path. Holy cow, the car is going to careen off the edge and fall hundreds of feet into the dark water below!

When the road ended, the lake spread out in front of us like an enormous azure tablecloth thrown across a summer picnic table. Tucked amongst a towering family of ancient evergreens, camouflaged in greens and browns and barely visible, was what appeared to be a house. The station wagon had barely come to a stop before the car doors flew open and we raced down a grassy hill toward the cottage.

It was a ranch style with weathered cedar shingles, a long narrow rectangular box with a sloping roof and rows and rows of windows. A matching screened in porch, lined with well used rockers, faced the water. Inside was typical lake house with an open area that provided an abundance of space for living, dining, and kitchen. Nothing all that fancy, but comfortable and functional with an unobstructed view of the lake. It was perfect.

Mother and Father met Mr. Smiley, an officer at the Chemung Canal Trust Company, signed the papers, and left with deed and warrantee in hand. The plan was that as soon as school was out, we would pack up and spend the warm months of summer at the lake. Dad traveling back and forth and Mom and Nannie holding down the fort during the week. Pa would make an occasional trek to his work but for the majority of the summer, he imagined himself sitting in one of the rockers on the front porch in a semi-retired state of euphoria.

So it was, with the car bulging with all of the necessities and much more, suitcases packed to overflowing with swim suits and shorts and jeans and sweaters, clothing for hot days and much cooler lake nights, pots and pans, sheets, pillow cases and comfy quilts, toys, decks of cards for playing crazy eights with Nannie and games like Monopoly and Scrabble and jigsaw puzzles. We were off.

This summer and for many summers thereafter, my life was all about the lake. It was Dad's mission that his eldest daughter would perfect her wilderness skills and become the consummate lake girl. I was officially in training, one might even call it boot camp. My father started this training with Angling 101. I would never become a lake girl unless I learned the basics of fishing. Many long hours were spent in a tiny aluminum boat bobbing up and down, and up and down and up and down on the oft times choppy lake. The most difficult of my assignments was not what you might think. It was not having to sit without moving a muscle. It was not having to be quiet as a little mouse. It was not about being patient. It was about the baiting of my own hook.

This was lesson number one when learning the art of angling and entailed digging to the bottom of a rusty old Maxwell House coffee can and pulling out a slimy, brownish angleworm. This was by no means an easy feat. These fat repulsive creatures somehow amassed themselves into one giant glob, under the layer of moist soil. The only way to retrieve one was to tug on one end until it was separated from its family. The problem was that after grabbing the head or tail (there's no way of knowing which was which) the worm would begin to writhe in my trembling hand, expanding and contracting like a crazed accordion at a polka party, curling around my fingers as it tried to escape my grasp. If this was not traumatic enough, I then had to further alienate this reluctant participant by piercing it with a very sharp barbed covered hook. Stabbing it not once but several times (depending on its length) until it resembled a tidy little worm knot. This was something that neither the worm nor I found particularly pleasurable.

After I finally accomplished this herculean task, I cast my line into the cold, dark water and with eyes fixed on the red and white plastic bobber that floated on the surface, I waited and waited and waited.

Mom would say that the only thing you could catch in Seneca Lake is a COLD.

My sister proved her wrong!

By the time August rolled around and the summer heat had made its presence known and the hint of cool that had once partnered with the summer breeze was conspicuously absent, it was time to find respite from the ninety plus temperatures in the always chilly, glacial waters of the lake. This sounds like the perfect solution for a cool down except that Seneca Lake was very cold, bone chilling cold and deep, very, very deep and from a kid's perspective, looked particularly menacing. To make matters worse, in order to get to the lake, I had to climb down a sheer cliff, down a series of narrow iron steps and at the bottom there was a conspicuous absence of a beach, just a wooden dock jutting out from a giant hunk of rock.

The perils of partaking in a lake swim did not end with the steep stairs or the limb numbing water, there was also the small inconvenience of snakes. Yes, this was an ideal habitat for water snakes. Snakes that called my little piece of paradise home, as well. They boldly sunned themselves on the warm rocky ledges and slithered through the water in a continuum of perfect S's. But Nannie had the reptilian situation well under control, by simply sitting on the edge of the dock, with an aluminum can filled with rocks at the ready, and at the slightest provocation hurled her earthen ammunition at the unsuspecting creature. I frolicked in the water trusting that my grandmother was on sentry duty, her eagle eye continuously scanning the water for even the slightest ripple.

My mother was a fish!

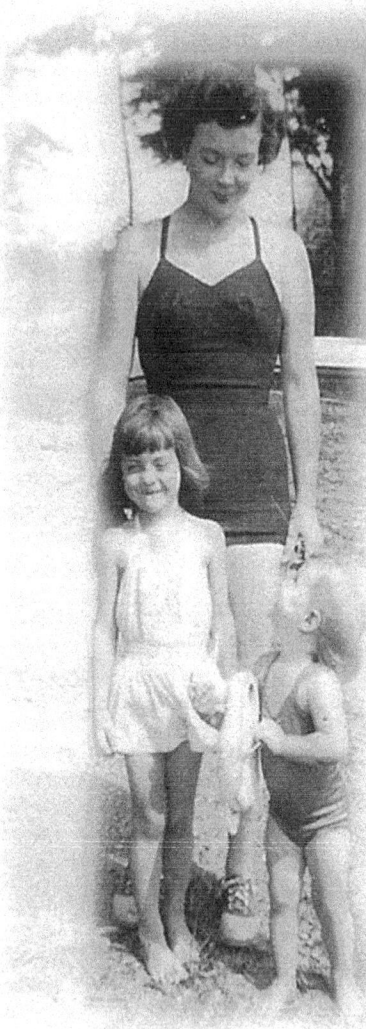

She could swim like no other human being. The back stroke, the breast stroke, butterfly, side stroke, she did them all. And she did them effortlessly without a hint of heavy breathing. When she slipped into the water she morphed from woman into trout or bass or marlin. Mom's lungs became gills and her legs moved as one scaleless flipper that propelled her through the water like a torpedo shot from the belly of a submarine. I did not inherit any of these aquatic attributes. First of all, I had no body mass. I was skinny as a rail and as soon as I hit the water, I would start gasping for air. Certainly, this time, I would drown. I would sink to the bottom like a lead pipe. It would be the end for me.

One afternoon, mother joined us on the dock, and for some ridiculous reason decided that I needed to learn how to dive. This idea seemed absolutely ludicrous. Why was it necessary for me to dive when it was far easier for me to just make my way down the wide wooden steps and into the cold dark water? Wasn't that enough? Wasn't that brave enough? But Mom was the boss, so I had no choice but to play along.

There I was shivering uncontrollably, not from the cold but from sheer terror. I was clinging to the edge of the dock like a fledgling raptor with toes wrapped in a death grip on the periphery. Shaking like a tambourine in a gypsy band with my mother, the sea nymph, effortlessly treading water below.

"Just bend your knees ever so slightly, stretch your arms out straight with your head down, take a deep, deep breath and push off with a bit of gusto." Sounds easy enough. I bent my knees, stretched out my arms, put my head down, took a gigantic big breath but the push off was problematic. The push off did not happen.

Regardless of my mother's pleading and prodding, sweet voice and not so sweet, I didn't budge. I didn't push off. I didn't dive. A million scenarios swirled in my head. The most prevalent one being the headlines in the next morning's Elmira Star Gazette "Little Girl Drowns in Seneca Lake." It was all too real. Too surreal. I was much too young to die. And Nannie told me that if you drowned in Seneca Lake, your body would be sucked into a huge cavernous hole and they would find you, days later, floating in the tiny lake in Eldridge Park, miles away in Elmira.

This is not the ending that I had planned but my mother was threatening to get out of the water and I knew what that meant. Quickly, I positioned myself and without looking back, bent my knees, put my head between my outstretched arms, and pushed with all my might. I hit the icy water and a blanket of frosty bubbles surrounded me, blurring my vision and filling my tiny lungs with a mixture that neither fish nor human could breathe, but I didn't drown. I didn't die. My mother grabbed me and pushed me to the surface where I was greeted with cheers and kudos and congratulatory "That's our girl!"

Lake life was all about challenges and experiences and facing one's fears. Communing with nature, roughing it, being able to adapt to a sometimes-solitary environment, was part and parcel of a summer spent at the cottage.

There were quiet times, when Nannie and Mom were busy. They might have been involved with a project or whipping up something delicious for dinner. They might be canning peaches from a nearby orchard or making homemade root beer all bubbly, warm, and yeasty.

And hectic times, when extended family came and the picnic table on the porch swelled to accommodate. Dad would throw more barbequed chicken on the grill, and more corn on the cob was husked and plunged into boiling water. More potato salad and more macaroni salad. Platters overflowed with slices of sweet, ripe tomatoes and cool, crunchy cucumber spears. Jars of homemade pickles and watermelon rind took their place along with carrot curls and celery sticks in a special relish dish that Nannie had brought from Herrick Street. Let us not forget dessert. Dessert, by the way, was not reserved for company; supper was just not complete without it. But when company came, Nannie and Mom pulled out the giant sheet pans for cakes; devil's food with chocolate buttercream icing, and yellow cake with seven-minute marshmallow frosting.

No summer picnic would be complete without slabs of icy, cold watermelon and pitchers of lemonade. What a feast.

Chapter Twenty-eight

Time Spent with My Nannie—more memories of the lake

Many nights at the cottage were spent curled up on my grandmother's lap reading books of tall tales about such folk heroes as Paul Bunyan and Johnnie Appleseed and the Pied Piper, reading old classics by Mark Twain and Dickens and Kipling and Defoe, or sweet poetry by Emily Dickinson or my all-time favorite poems of the villainous blood curdling Edgar Allan Poe.

Nannie also loved telling me stories about our ancestors who came to America from Ireland to escape religious oppression and the potato famine. She told me stories of back breaking work in the coal mines of Pennsylvania, bawdy, barroom fights brought on by talk of religion or politics or too much whiskey.

When the nights became too warm inside the cottage, we would escape to the screened in front porch where the lapping of the waves and the tiniest hint of a breeze made it the perfect place to float away to faraway lands. Exotic places with parrot filled jungles and deserts, with ghost like sheiks, on snorting, prancing equines racing across the dunes. When we weren't in the mood for adventure, we would simply sit and rock, content with counting the hundreds of lightning bugs that lit up the yard like Japanese lanterns crisscrossing the darkness. All of this was accompanied by a chorus of crickets and at times cicadas, all competing to have their message heard above the fray. This had to be the noisiest peaceful place on Earth.

On the weekend when Dad was at the lake, we would all gather around the fire pit in the backyard and toast marshmallows. My father would cut a slender bough perfect for the task at hand. I was allowed, with parental supervision, to commandeer my grandfather's Swiss Army knife and whittle a pointy tip on one end of the stick that would secure the sugary confection as it dangled over the hot coals. Now, there was most definitely established protocol to follow while toasting marshmallows. Most important, the marshmallow must never catch on fire, no matter how tempting. To prevent this from happening, one had to be constantly vigilant, keeping the stick in a state of perpetual motion. Rotating the marshmallow as if it were a rogue planet circling the campfire sun.

Perfection could not be rushed, could not be hurried, there were no shortcuts.

Chapter Twenty-nine

Waiting for Mom and Dad—as recounted to me by Nannie and Mom

It was autumn, sometime in the early 1950's, when my mother and father were summoned to a trailer park in Sarasota, Florida where my Grandmother H had lived for many years. Some sort of family business that, at the time, I was not made privy to. They were going to be gone for ten days and Nannie and Pa came to our house so that our school schedule would not be disrupted. I was sure that this would mean a much later bedtime, a fresh batch of oatmeal raisin cookies every day, and if by total accident, I happened to get my Mary Jane's wet on my way home from school, no big deal.

Thankfully, that was exactly the way it was. The ten days flew by and before I knew it, Mom and Dad had left Florida and were heading north. They would be home in three days and we all couldn't wait to see them. I couldn't wait to see them.

The phone call came in the middle of the night, jarring everyone in the house into a sleepy awake. There were heavy footsteps heard rushing down the upstairs hallway and then down the stairs to the phone in the kitchen.

It wasn't until morning that Nannie and Pa revealed the message of the middle of the night phone call. Dad was in the hospital. That was about all the information that was shared on the onset. It was only after several days of eavesdropping on my grandparents' conversations (Nannie called it a child with "big ears") that I began to learn what had happened.

Mom and Dad had left Sarasota and were heading north. Dad was driving and Mom was riding shot gun. They had just crossed the Florida-Georgia border when my father felt a stabbing pain in his stomach and was terribly nauseous and chilled. His countenance had taken on a frightening, pasty pallor and sweat dripped from his forehead. Sweat that ran down the sides of his face like someone had just turned on the spigot. Mother morphed from wife to nurse and assuming he had picked up a flu bug, wrapped him in a blanket and took over the driving.

She planned on stopping in the next town to find a drug store for some Pepto. Pepto Bismol would help with the nausea and he could sleep and be better in the morning. As she drove, she kept one eye on the road and another on her husband who was still rolled up in the fetal position in the back seat, still shaking from the chills. Still the color of concrete, his hair matted with perspiration. Still curled up like a roly-poly when you poke it with a stick. None of this was good. When Mother finally saw the sign that said, Jessup 28 miles, she knew that this was far more than the flu and she had to find a hospital post haste. She gripped the steering wheel tightly in hopes that her hands would stop shaking and pressed the gas pedal to the floor. She thought that maybe the speeding station wagon with New York tags would attract the attention of a Georgia State Police officer. They had seen many, earlier in the day, lying in wait for an unsuspecting traveler in a little too much of a hurry. She sped along the interstate counting down the miles. Twenty-seven...twenty-six...twenty-five... She was so hypnotized by the rolling numbers on the odometer that she never saw the blue lights swirling behind her. It wasn't until the piercing screech of the siren yanked her back to reality that she realized that she might be getting a ticket for speeding and that her prayers had been answered. Luck would have it that the hospital was close by and now my mother was chasing the blue lights of the squad car as she followed the officer, who not only was escorting her to the hospital but had radioed ahead so that the emergency room staff would be given a heads up.

Ready they were. As Mom approached the hospital entrance, still glued to the police car in the lead, she headed towards the looming blue white "Emergency Room" sign that announced that they had indeed arrived. Mother had barely gotten the car into park when the double doors magically opened and two orderlies, pushing a stretcher, approached the car. Without a word, they pulled my father from the back seat, put him on the stretcher and charged through the glass doors, only to disappear into the belly of a stark white, antiseptic hallway. When the doors slammed behind them, stenciled on the doors was a sign that read "Authorized Personnel Only."

The next several hours were spent filling out admission's forms and waiting. Waiting for some news, waiting for the metal doors to open, waiting for someone in a white coat to appear with a kind face and reassuring tone, waiting to hear that her husband was going to be okay. Word came with a gentle tap on her shoulder and a soft southern accent murmuring her name. Somehow, she had fallen into a troubled sleep, too exhausted from the events of the day to keep her eyes open. She was led through a maze of white walls until she came to a small office. An office with a wooden desk and two well-worn chairs and boxes and boxes of patient files. The shelves were crammed with medical publications and reference books and journals and such. The walls were decorated with framed diplomas from medical school and certificates of accomplishments and licenses to practice in the State of Georgia. Wide awake now, Mom stared at the wall, reading the name of the doctor and wondering what news he might have. She was brought back to the present by the sound of footsteps approaching the office.

Dr. Jonathon Ramsey had been on call that night and had wasted no time getting my father into the operating room. He feared that his patient had acute appendicitis and even more concerned that the appendix might have ruptured, a very serious, possibly life-threatening condition. After a brief introduction and a quick exchange of pleasantries, he explained that Dad's appendix had indeed ruptured and peritonitis had set in. He was relieved that the young wife of his newest patient was a registered nurse and fully understood the ramifications of what he was saying.

It would be a long, most assuredly, rocky road to recovery, a wait and see of trying to fight the infection that had spread all too quickly. Dad was moved to a room on the third floor of the surgical wing and preparations were made for my mother to stay in the room with him. A small cot was placed in the corner under a set of windows that provided her with a view of the Georgia countryside and when opened allowed a stream of real air to mix with the stale mix of septic and sickness. Quickly she morphed from wife to nurse, efficiently organizing their tiny space so that she could take the very best care of her now very ill husband.

Hours had become days and days had become weeks. Mother had become a fixture at the small rural hospital. A member of the staff on the third floor, the head nurse in room 309. Except for an occasional scurry to the small coffee shop in the main lobby, she was her husband's constant companion, her omnipresence, her strength, her persistence was noticed by all who ventured into her domain.

Yet despite all of the efforts by the medical staff and all of the care provided by Mother and many others, there were no signs that Dad was getting better. He was still extremely weak, his eyes had taken on a yellowish jaundice like tint and charcoal gray circles spread from his lower lids down his cheeks in perfect semicircles. He was still running a temperature, he was not eating, and his already tall lanky frame was looking more and more skeleton-like with every passing day. The outline of his diminished self, showed through the white muslin sheet that was tucked neatly around him. The poison from the ruptured appendix was not the least bit intimidated by the medication that was being furiously pumped into him from a long serpent like tube. A tube that carried the pharmaceutical cocktail from a

116

large plastic bag into an IV that was meticulously taped to my father's arm.

Mother was not at all surprised when the doctor delivered the grim news. It might be time for my grandparents to bring the children to see their father. However, before my mother made the call, she decided to first contact a doctor from the hospital where she had gotten her training. A doctor who was highly regarded, a brilliant practitioner, and someone who my mother prayed might have a solution. My father needed a miracle and a miracle was about to happen. A drug that had just been released by the FDA, might be just the long-awaited remedy. It might be the cure that would save my father's life. It might be the answer to my mother's prayers. It was called Tetramyacin, dubbed a wonder drug and certainly worth a try.

It was almost as if someone snapped their fingers and my father was on the road to recovery. One day Dad was gravely ill and the next, he was sitting up in bed taking nourishment, rosy cheeked and filled with piss and vinegar.

Our travel plans were shelved, my grandparents settled back into their routine as caregivers to their two young granddaughters and life returned to a semi state of normalcy. There was school, dinner at exactly five o'clock, feeding the dog, helping Nannie dry the dishes and putting the silverware in their designated slot. There was an eight o'clock bedtime story and prayers before all lights were out. There were piano lessons, listening to the radio sitting next to my Pa, and on the weekend a trip to Herrick Street or shopping or just playing outside until the streetlights flickered.

Several weeks passed before we finally got word that Dad was well enough to travel. Pa wanted to fly to Jessup and drive my parents back to New York but mother, knowing that finances had been stretched to the limit and that an airline ticket would come with a hefty price tag, assured her anxious parents that she was more than capable and totally comfortable making the journey home. She had poured over the giant Texaco road map, making a red line along US 1 from Georgia, up the eastern coast through South and North Carolina, through the lovely, cool, rolling hills of Virginia, then Maryland and finally the homestretch, Pennsylvania and New York.

An entourage of nurses and orderlies and ladies from the cafeteria and even some of the janitorial staff had gathered at the front of the hospital to say their goodbyes. My parents had become a part of the tiny rural hospital's family and with my father's miraculous recovery, had taken on an almost celebrity-like status. They all crowded around the young couple as the candy striper helped my dad into the awaiting car. When the engine began to hum and the whole car started to shake in anticipation of their long journey, everyone shouted their well wishes. They waved goodbye as my mother, with her husband wrapped in a hospital blanket by her side, disappeared down the long winding driveway and out of sight.

Mother was amazingly calm and quite confident that the trip home, with the help of her handy road map, was going to be uneventful and so it was. Dad snoozed on and off and when awake did his best to help her with directions and keep her from becoming lulled into the monotony of hours of driving.

They tried to time their stop each night so that they didn't have to be in the car for more than eight hours. But suitable lodging was not always available and there were times when towns were hundreds of miles apart and civilization was reserved for the wild beasts of the never-ending forests and horses and cattle that grazed on thousands of acres of fertile farmland.

When they did find a place to spend the night, it was usually at a mom and pop motel. Motels with names like Shady Acres or Sleepy Inn or Mountain View and they had few amenities aside from the fact that they were clean and tidy and on a trip like this clean and tidy was just what they needed.

On the third day, they became very aware that the flatness of the South and the soft rise of elevation beyond the South was morphing into some serious mountainous terrain. There was no doubt about it, they were in Pennsylvania and as the adage goes...they could smell the barn. They were almost home. They were trying their hardest to push through, but they had already been driving for more than ten hours and Mom was exhausted. The winding road that had been a challenge before the sun disappeared was now almost impossible to navigate as darkness swallowed them up like a giant gray whale. Mom popped on the high beams while Dad scanned the blackness to his right, anxious to spot even the slightest glimmer of light. Light from a distant farmhouse or an old gas station or possibly the flickering light of a vacancy sign. And finally, there it was, a light. Indistinguishable at first, but like a moth to a flame, the car was drawn to it until at last a unanimous whoop exploded from the weary travelers and Dad could finally make out the sign "The Green Valley Motor Lodge". Yes, this would be a perfect place for them to spend the night.

You might have thought that Mother would have fallen in bed never to awaken but that was not the case. She tossed and turned, and turned and tossed, flipping her pillow like a blackjack dealer flipping his cards. She stared at the ceiling, she stared at her sleeping husband, she crawled out of bed and stared out the front windows of their room. Everyone and everything on planet Earth were fast asleep even their old station wagon seemed to be in dreamland.

The night seemed like it would never end, and day light came way too soon. It was back in the car and after a quick cup of coffee, compliments of the motel night manager, they were off.

Nannie insisted that I jump in the bathtub and get the dirt and grime and kid smell off me. The party was over, my parents were coming home, the Nannie rules were about to be replaced by the Mom and Dad rules. My grandmother informed me that I would be wearing a dress and quickly braided my hair covering the rubber bands with matching plaid ribbons. Nannie loved braids because in her exact words, "They keep all that messy hair out of your eyes." I didn't understand the big deal but I was willing to cooperate for once. And to be honest two of my all-time cowgirl heroes were Calamity Jane and Annie Oakley and they both had long hair and on occasion wore ungirlie girl braids. Sans the plaid ribbons.

I was then shooed out the front door to act as sentry at the end of the driveway. I paced back and forth, never taking my eyes off the road, waiting to see the station wagon chugging up Lovell Avenue. As soon as it was spotted, I was supposed to run full speed back down the driveway and into the house to alert my grandparents. After all, that's what a sentry does. Nannie was quite explicit, "When you see the car get back here lickety-split." I assured her that I would not let her down. Of course, I could have done a much better job as her scout if I had been allowed to wear my cowgirl outfit but I was determined to make the best of it.

I'm certainly not trying to make excuses... but. Things started to unravel when I decided that I just couldn't possibly wait at the end of the driveway and instead, made my way to the bottom of the hill by cutting through a stand of pine trees. It was just plain bad luck when at the exact same time that I was making my mad dash, my parents turned the corner and were heading up the hill. I assume that Nannie must have heard my screams and got to the end of the driveway just in time to see my parents' car sputtering up the hill and her granddaughter running behind the car, arms flailing, pigtails flapping in the wind, her tooth pick legs pumping like a marathoner and shouting...

"Mom, Dad, WAIT! STOP!"

Chapter Thirty
A Day at Eldridge Park—me and my Nannie

Nannie and Pa had their suitcases loaded into their car before the sun set behind the giant blue spruce in the front yard. Something about they wanted to get home before dark or some such nonsense. I guess this was understandable considering that they had come for what they thought would be ten days and wound up staying for weeks. Understandably, they had been through a very trying period and were anxious to get back to Herrick Street.

We all crowded into the doorway where we waved goodbye, we blew kisses, and yelled "I love you!" When the car had completely disappeared, with not even a glimmer from the headlights and the dust had all but settled, we realized that we were all still standing in the doorway, still staring at the empty driveway like we were just waking up from a long, long dreadful dream.

The next morning, I realized that even though my parents were home, things were not back to normal and I had a ton of questions for my mother. Why were they gone so long? What happened to Dad? Why is he still in bed? Is he going to die? And most importantly who is going to take me to school?

Within a matter of a couple of weeks, Dad was back to work and indeed, my father was taking me to school. Things were back to normal; our routine ala Mom and Dad was being implemented without exception. I dressed quickly in the morning without whining, I ate those disgusting yellow wax beans that Dad loved with just a bit of gagging and bedtime was at eight o'clock.

On the weekend, Nannie took me to Herrick Street to give Mom a bit of a reprieve and give the two of us some time together. It had been a perfect spring and the weather was Chamber of Commerce delightful. Sunny but not too warm. The rains were considerate enough to happen in the middle of the night so that everyone's yard was a carpet of emerald green. Alas, all the tulips and iris and daffodils made a lovely rainbow of pastel colors that arched along the periphery of Nannie's garden on the side of the house. We would be out in the yard at the first crack of daylight, pulling weeds, aerating the soil with this strange tool with prongy things on the end, raking up grass cuttings that Pa had missed when he mowed, and watering anything and everything that looked even the slightest bit thirsty.

As soon as Nannie was satisfied that her yard was again the cause for rampant neighborhood envy and jealousy, we headed inside to get cleaned up for a day of fun. One of my most favorite things to do was to go to Eldridge Park.

Eldridge Park was every kid's nirvana, it was heaven, it was an amusement park like no other. Where does one begin? Let's start with the nucleus, the center, the hub, the merry-go-round. I loved, loved, loved the merry-go-round. It was breathtaking, at first glance, with the giant snarling jungle cats and wild horses with tails and manes unfurled. Each one painted in brilliant circus colors, like cobalt blue and sunflower yellow and ruby scarlet red and a heavy-handed swath of gold and silver. Each beast frozen, as if petrified in their particular terrifying pose, rearing on their hind legs or crouching ready to pounce at any unsuspecting child naïve enough to wander too close. And there was music. The calliope whistled to the tune of Oom-Pah-Pah, Oom-Pah-Pah.

When Nannie first brought me to Eldridge Park, I was too young to ride on the merry-go-round by myself, so my grandmother would pick me up, carry me to the platform and with impeccable timing, we'd leap onto the still moving carousel. I would slide into the saddle and wrap my arms around the shiny brass pole, as my great stallion shimmied up and down to the rhythm of the blaring organ music.

The long-awaited sign of coming of age, for me, was to ride solo, without adult accompaniment, without my grandmother. On that infamous, never to be forgotten day, I knew that I was ready. I was ready to make my merry-go-round debut. Nannie was nervous but I assured her that her fears were for naught. It was my fait accompli that, in what seemed like a millisecond of eternities, I went from platform, to spinning top, to mounting one of the galloping, wild, wooden beasts.

Unfortunately, I still had to watch, with agonizing envy, as the big kids leaned as far out of their saddles as humanly possible and with arms outstretched, tried to grab the gold ring. Let me explain. There was a ladder like contraption that had been erected about fifteen or twenty feet from the platform. Perched on top, on a wooden bench, sat a park employee who fed metal rings down a chute. The challenge was that as you whirled around, while going up and down, you had to snatch a ring from this metal arm that for many, including myself, was just out of reach. Hence, the need to lean out, without tumbling out, in order to grab the illusive ring. To make this whole process even more exciting, during each ride, there would be one gold ring. If you were lucky enough to snag that one and show it to the attendant, next time you rode for free. A free ride but more importantly, bragging rights. It just doesn't get any better than that.

Directly across from the merry-go-round was the Whip. As its name denotes, the Whip consisted of about twenty, two-man stationary cars on a circular track. When all the cars were full and the attendant had checked all the safety straps, he would give the signal for the operator to push the giant metal lever that set everything in motion. When the ride was activated, all the cars took a sudden leap forward and building momentum, began to spin around faster and faster and faster. So fast that the wind in my face made my eyes water like standing under a garden hose. This ride defied all scientific laws of physics, defying force and inertia. The riders were hurled in a clockwise direction and then suddenly, with a huge jolt, reversed course and spun in the other direction. Nannie refused to go on this ride with me so I would not be riding on the Whip on this day. I would have to wait for a time that one of my parents was available.

Looming over the entire park was a giant wooden roller coaster. Miles and miles of ribbon like metal track circled the landscape. This ride was definitely not for the faint of heart. Cars that were strung together in a conga line of potential catastrophe, trudged up the first incline at an alarming seventy-degree angle. Click, click, click, click, click. I could hear the metal clasps trying their best to hold the overloaded cars from sliding backward off the tracks. When the first car finally reached the summit, its sheer weight and gravity hurled all that followed at a breakneck speed, down the other side. Of course, standing up in the car during its downward plunge was strictly forbidden. However, there were always those very brave or very foolish souls (more than likely teenagers who were trying to impress someone) who would wave their arms in the air while emitting blood curdling screams. Screams that were part ecstasy and part adrenalin rush with a healthy dose of unimaginable terror. I could not bring myself to attempt this dare devilish stunt and preferred to maintain my death grip on the bar for fear that the sheer force of it would eject me from my seat and I would plummet to the ground like Isaac Newton's apple.

This would be the perfect time for me to mention that my mother was covered from head to toes with a beautiful, brownish, red blanket of freckles. Freckles that she absolutely abhorred, until one particular day. It all happened when we were on our second or third ride on the roller coaster. A fresh young lad, who was strapping us in for another whirl around the track, mentioned to Mom that if he could guess how many freckles she had, our next ride was free. Tongue in cheek, his guess was a million gazillion and Mother retorted, "How did you know?" and off we went.

After all the excitement of the rides, it was time to replenish ourselves with a not so healthy dose of sucrose. At Eldridge Park, sugar reigned and grease held a position of prominence. All you had to do was stroll down the alley way behind the merry-go-round to find rows of booths all hawking their wares of something sweet and something gooey and something fried and something greasy.

Let's begin with sweet. There was one such booth that was nothing more than a wooden box on wheels. Its sides were adorned with larger than life depictions of what could be yours for pennies. Colorful pictures of a candied apple on a stick, cotton candy spun onto a paper cone, popcorn all drippy with butter, and soda pop in cola, orange and grape flavors. The front of the booth was glass so that all of this deliciousness was on full display, a devilish sales tactic as how could any red-blooded American kid resist any of these tempting treats? The question begged, "Which one should I choose?"

I was instantly drawn to the candied apples. After all, they were so beautiful, almost too beautiful to eat. Like Dorothy's ruby red slippers in The Wizard of Oz, they exuded their redness all shimmering and glossy, so shiny that they looked wet. The challenge was breaking through its, hard as a rock, candy armor that guarded the juicy slightly tart apple inside. I had perfected a positively brilliant plan of attack. I would tilt my head at a forty-five degree angle to said candied apple and sink my eye tooth into the vulnerable shell that I had been licking with this tactic in mind. It was pretty much foolproof. It worked every time.

But maybe the cotton candy would be more to my liking. It definitely was less of a challenge to eat, actually it was no challenge at all. As a matter of fact, as soon as you touched it with your tongue, it turned from a fluffy, lighter than air confection to a gummy, sugary wad, like an unrecognizable form of matter not yet discovered by scientists. Moreover, the process of making cotton candy was fascinating. There was a large metal tub that had some kind of motorized gizmo inside. The vendor would pour a rainbow stream of colored sugar into the center of the tub and then turn it on. From that point on the whole process is something of a mystery, as I was much too short to see inside the tub. Somehow, with the magic of whirling hot air, the crystals of sugar became filmy sheets of sweet that were twirled around and around on a paper cone until it could hold no more. The final product looked like some crazy bouffant hair style in psychedelic colors. Eating this was also a bit tricky because of the sticky factor. Maybe the Sno-cone or the buttery popcorn or the corn dog on a stick or frozen custard would be the better choice.

With a full belly and a sugar saturated brain, I was ready to take on the bumper cars. This thrill producing ride was simple in its concept. You hopped into a Keystone Cops kind of jalopy that was perched atop a ring of rubber tire. The objective was to crash into the other cars that were in turn, trying to smash into you. What could be more fun? There was a quasi-gas pedal for speed and a steering wheel to maneuver your vehicle into striking position. The rest was easy. You merely chose your target. You tried to pick someone who looked like a newbie, the one who was gripping the steering wheel for dear life or better yet screaming for his mom to get him off. You then pressed on the gas pedal with all your might, smashing into the side of his car. The only problem was that you might become the unsuspecting victim. The target for malice and destruction, by some unknown assailant who was gunning for you.

When Nannie had enough of all the screeching and screaming and indiscriminate crashing, it was off to the arcade. The arcade, so civilized, so not heart thumping nor adrenaline producing. Where the screeching, crashing, and screaming, was replaced by flashing rainbow lights and the ping, ping, ping of the pinball machines.

My favorite was the skeet ball machines, where you rolled wooden balls (five for a nickel) up an incline to score points. At the top of the incline there was a series of holes, think dart board with the small center hole being worth the most points. I think that the center hole was worth one hundred points and each adjoining ring would be worth fifty, then twenty, then ten. If your ball did not make it to the top, you received no points for that ball. You got nothing, zero, zipparoo. Everyone had their own technique which included banking your ball at just the right spot, body English, popping your ball off the mesh netting, and a crazy back handed approach that put a wicked spin on the ball. The latter being my own personal favorite that I learned from Dad who fancied himself a skeet ball professional, a skeet ball connoisseur. He was quite the role model and when I was playing skeet ball with my father, I always felt like the luckiest kid on the planet. One's reward for all this tomfoolery was displayed on a chalk board above the row of skeet ball machines for the whole world to see. "SKEET BALL HIGH SCORE 450" and then your name scrawled in grease pencil in giant capital letters.

Bragging rights.

Chapter Thirty-one

From Humble Beginnings—the best memories

Elmira, New York was a small and yet bustling city in the mid nineteen fifties. Its growth fed by a booming manufacturing sector, fueled by companies like American Bridge, General Electric, American LaFrance, Westinghouse and Remington Rand. The vast majority of people worked on the assembly lines. Blue collar workers, who manned the conveyor belts, did the same monotonous task over and over again, for as many years as they were able to show up and punch the time clock. These jobs afforded them a decent living. They were able to provide for their families, buy a house and partake in the American dream. Not to be overlooked, was the promise of job security. Companies took care of and valued their employees and there were strong labor unions that made sure that they did.

Life was quiet, life was uncomplicated. Neighborhoods grew at the same pace as the city center. The neighborhood to the south, where my grandparents lived on Herrick Street, was called the South Side and was home to many of the factory workers, store clerks and salesmen, shopkeepers and teachers. People whose roots spread like a giant elm from Great Britain and Eastern Europe across the Atlantic to their new country, confident that their children would have a better life. People whose parents had spoken Gaelic and Polish and German and Italian. Waves of impoverished refugees, like my great-great grandparents, had come to the U.S. from Ireland because of the devastating effects of the potato famine and religious intolerance.

It was understandable that from their working-class roots, my grandparents believed very firmly in the principles of the Protestant work ethic and living within ones means. The latter was never more evident than how I was entertained. My grandmother had learned, at an early age that "A penny saved was a penny earned." Those times, when Nannie and I were together, were rich in togetherness but were minimal in terms of cost.

To mention just a few: Saturday afternoon was spent catching a movie downtown at the Strand Theatre. The three-hour-long matinee cost but a nickel, and even though we passed the mile-long refreshment counter, we were not stopping. I could catch only a glimpse of the neatly stacked boxes of Jujubes, Raisonettes, Necco Wafers, Sno Caps, and black licorice gum drops called Crows. Not to be ignored, there was popcorn. Deliciously buttery, fresh from the popper, popcorn. The mere sight of the exploding kernels and then the unmistakable smell was almost too much to resist. But Nannie was not about to spend her hard- earned money on such an extravagance and instead had popped our popcorn at home and shoveled it into a large brown paper bag. She would then wrap it in her sweater as we hurried through the lobby and when the lights went down in the theatre, it would magically appear with no one the wiser.

A typical Saturday matinee featured the news of the week, cartoons starring Bugs Bunny and Elmer Fudd, Donald Duck and his nephews Huey, Dewey and Louie and the oh so cute, Daisy Duck. I'm not sure about the relationship of

Donald and Daisy or where the parents of the three nephews were but in 1952 you didn't ask about such things.

My all-time favorite was Sylvester, the feline with the lovable lisp and his insatiable quest to make Tweety Bird, a plump little canary, his dinner. In every episode, Tweety Bird would be innocently sitting in his cage, totally unaware of the impending danger. As Sylvester slinked toward his unsuspecting victim, I would be terrified, imagining the most terrible of outcomes for the precious little bird. The closer that the cat got to the cage, the more anxious I became. Squirming in my seat, screaming to myself "Tweety, The CAT is going to eat you!" Until finally, not being able to watch any longer, I would throw my sweater over my head, stick my fingers in my ears and wait until it was safe to come out. Of course, Sylvester was never able to eat Tweety Bird and in the end, he would sulk off with his all too familiar words of disappointment and disgust "Suffering Succotash!"

Then it was time for the feature film, and I was never disappointed if it was one of my favorite western movies. There I would be, atop my galloping steed, lost in a perpetual cloud of prairie dust and the clamor of hooves, in wild pursuit of the bad guys that had just rustled some cattle from the Circle A ranch. There were the good guys in tall white Stetsons and the bad guys in black. There was always a moral to the story; right always prevailed over wrong and the good guys always won. Always. Welcome to life in the 1950s.

On very special occasions, we were treated to the magic of Walt Disney with all the adventure and excitement that a kid might dream of. However, all the Disney movies came with one caveat. All Disney movies were sad, heartbreaking sad, so sad that you had to bury your face in your grandmother's lap, sad. Cinderella had her ugly stepsisters. Dumbo the elephant was teased because of his extra-large ears. Snow White was tricked into eating a poison apple.

But, by far, the saddest of all Disney movies was Bambi. Bambi was particularly traumatic because the unthinkable happened…. his mother was shot and killed. What possibly could be any worse? Losing one's mother was impossible to reconcile in the eyes of an eight-year-old. Nannie held me tight in anticipation of the impending tragedy. With her hand in her coat pocket, she was ready to retrieve her oversized starched hankie to mop up my tears. After all, it was just a movie.

Nannie loved to take my sister and me to the many state parks in Central New York and there was an abundance of them. One of my favorites was Enfield Glen which was a short drive from Elmira. My grandmother had purchased an old jalopy from a local used car dealer and although we still took the bus to town, her new-found wheels gave us an opportunity for some exploration.

Enfield Glen was tucked into a remote, pine filled, recreation area where enormous rock cliffs cantilevered over a narrow path that hugged the hillside to the very popular swimming hole.

My grandmother would pack a picnic basket for the perfect lunch in the woods. There were cream cheese and strawberry jelly sandwiches on white bread, apples and oranges, carrot strips and radishes (with a tiny wax paper packet of salt for dipping) raisin oatmeal cookies and my grandfather's old thermos filled with lemonade.

Picnic tables dotted the trail and it was my job to find the perfect spot. Not too much shade...not too much sun and I had to make sure that the table was somewhat clean, nothing sticky or gooey and no bird poop! That was very important. When the ideal spot was decided on, Nannie would rummage through the basket and pull out the well-worn red and white checkered plastic tablecloth. Lunch was spread out like a grand feast and we eagerly cleaned up every last drop of anything that was edible. Hiking sure makes a kid hungry.

After everything was tidied up, it was off again along the trail until we got to the swimming hole. The voices of happy swimmers could be heard as we marched closer. The unmistakable sounds of kids laughing and splashing and shouting to their moms, "Hey Mom, watch this! Watch me! Watch me!" as they cannonballed off the high diving board.

There was a long row of dressing rooms before we got to the water where we had to change into our bathing suits and this was always problematic. Understand, that there was only a flimsy curtain to provide some semblance of privacy as I changed. A flimsy curtain, that Nannie at times forgot to close tightly, was all that there was to protect me from some gawking stranger that might just be passing by.

It didn't seem to matter how much I protested. She simply did not understand my trepidations, my plight, my concerns pertaining to modesty and privacy. I guess this should not have been so surprising considering that I was just a scrawny, skinny kid. So if I dawdled, digging in my heels, she would take matters into her own hands by quickly pulling off any remaining clothes and holding my bathing suit out in front of me, the leg holes beckoning and within a millisecond it was on and I was properly covered.

The swimming hole itself was a monster. A midnight blue abyss that was most likely formed when enormous glaciers pushed their way through this region during the Ice Age. Glaciers that scraped the earth's surface exposing huge chunks of sedimentary rock that formed walls of shimmering shale that lined the water's edge. There was a series of stone ledges that rimmed the entire basin making it the perfect spot for the cautious beginner who could sit on the second step and pretend swim until they felt confident enough to take the plunge into the black as night icy cold water. For the experienced swimmer, there was plenty of deep water to explore, far away from all the screeching toddlers who were clinging to their mothers. On a very warm summer's day there could be a hundred people bobbing and floating and trying to escape the heat of a typical July afternoon and not a single swimmer would feel intruded upon. There were four lifeguard stands, strategically placed, that loomed like giant sentry posts. Each occupied by teenage boys who all fit the same description...tall, a bit muscle bound, sunglasses, hair that had been bleached by day's spent on their perches, tanned to a golden glow accentuated by a generous slathering of Coppertone, and finally zinc oxide, all white, on the bridge of their noses.

I know for a fact, that they didn't notice me but I certainly noticed them. I was fascinated, mesmerized by their every move. All of this had to go on under the watchful eye of my grandmother. I had to be coy. I had to be nonchalant. I had to play it cool. How embarrassing it would be if she ever suspected. I did take solace in the fact that she was way too old to ever catch on to any of my romantic notions. After all, I was pretty sure that on her next birthday she was going to be fifty-four. As was mentioned, nothing to worry about.

At the far end, also the deepest end of the swimming hole, stood the diving board. A towering wooden edifice that sent many a chill up the spine of the timid, the young, the inexperienced. I remember sitting next to Nannie on our blanket and watching the big kids climb up the iron ladder. I would try to imagine the thrill of making that journey, walking to the end of the diving board and without hesitation, throwing myself off the end and somersaulting into the water below. Breathing air one minute and blowing streams of frothy bubbles out of my nose the next. Struggling to get to the surface and just when I was almost out of oxygen, I was there. I was looking quite cool, calm and collected as I reached for the, all too welcome, rock ledge and terra firma. Nothing to it.

Well, that's almost the way that it happened. I started up the ladder when suddenly, my legs started shaking so badly that I didn't think they could hold up the scrawny rest of me. I considered suffering the humiliation of backing down the ladder, but there was already someone on the rung behind me and several others behind him. I pushed on. When I finally reached the top, I ordered my feet to move to the end of the board and they reluctantly obeyed. There was now a long line of divers lined up waiting their turn. I had to go. I don't remember much after that except that the water was really cold when I finally made impact. The dive was nondescript but at least it wasn't a belly flopper and I made it back to the blanket without breaking down completely. My grandmother didn't say a word. She wrapped me in my towel and went along with my little charade that I was shivering from the icy water and most certainly not because I was scared out of my wits.

My secrets were always safe with her.

Chapter Thirty-two

My Nannie Was Rich—how she pulled the wool over my eyes

There was always an abundance of everything at Nannie's house. That's just the way it was supposed to be. While my mother would say "No dessert until you eat your green beans" my grandmother would say "Of course you can have another helping of rice pudding." Aside from the jam-packed refrigerator filled with delicious food, her kitchen counter, next to the oven, always had an apple pie or chocolate chip cookies cooling. To keep me busy, while all of this baking was going on, there were stacks of coloring books and a giant box of Crayola crayons. Not the cheapy box like I had in school. The one with silver and gold and burnt umber and peach and fuchsia.

There was an old cedar chest, in the upstairs hallway, stuffed to overflowing, with my large collection of dolls. Even a western rough riding cowgirl, like me, enjoyed an afternoon out of the saddle, all curled up on her grandmother's sewing room floor. There were dolls of all shapes and sizes, some soft and cuddly, others made of plastic with curly blonde tresses. I was especially fond of my curvaceous "pre Barbie" dolls that Nannie spent hours making clothes for. She was an accomplished seamstress who could make her vintage Singer sewing machine purr like a kitten just by pushing up and down on the treadle. The treadle being a labor-intensive metal grate that she would pump with her feet. No electricity needed. Her nimble fingers worked the tiny pieces of fabric through the bobbing needle as she rocked the treadle back and forth.

The remnants from past sewing projects came to life as tiny evening dresses and faux fur wraps, tweed suits and silky blouses and pajamas made from scraps of flannel. It was magical and my grandmother was the magician.

Each year, right after Thanksgiving, dolls from my collection would mysteriously disappear only to reappear on Christmas morning. There they would be, tucked under the tree, all decked out in their new holiday finery, ala Nannie.

Probably, my favorite doll in the whole wide world was a giant rag doll, that my grandmother made, named Brownie. The name synonymous with the color of her hair. Not terribly original but fitting. She also sewed Brownie's twin sister, for my sister, that we called Blondie. Yes, you guessed it, she was the one with blonde hair. As always, I got the doll that matched my hair and my sister got the one that matched hers. I was all right with that, sort of, but just once I would have liked something blond and blue eyed. A doll dressed in something pink and frilly instead of a doll with brown hair and brown eyes in an outfit of forest green plaid. Not that I was unhappy with my mousy, scrawny, cow-eyed tom-girl self. There were things in life that you just didn't have any control over. Things that you couldn't change. And it was unthinkable that I might be envious of my chubby little sister with platinum locks and sparkling blue eyes. I always thought that she was absolutely, positively adorable. But maybe just once, there might be something pastel and not plaid.

Blondie and Brownie were enormous, probably close to three feet tall. Their torsos, heads, arms and legs were made from soft cotton material, stuffed with a squishy batten filler that made them very huggable and the perfect sleeping companions. Which was a very good thing as I hated sleeping alone and I could not convince my sister to leave her room.

The hands and feet were little cloth balls with digits made with needle and thread. Nannie sewed the faces with red, blue, brown and black yarn and, of course, yellow and brown yarn for their hair. She always made sure to leave the hair long enough for the occasional braid or ponytail. Blondie and Brownie came with an extensive wardrobe of dresses and skirts, PJ's and lounge wear and even a strapless evening gown.

Not only were our dolls ready to meet Prince Charming at the ball, but so were my sister and me. Under the tree, we found matching evening gowns. Full length and strapless, they were fashioned from the most luxurious satin fabric and in the same steel blue color as our dolls' gowns. I knew that Santa Claus didn't bring Brownie down the chimney, but it really didn't matter to me, she was hands down the best Christmas present that I ever got.

Satin Dolls

Nannie was a whiz on her sewing machine. She could make big people's clothes and little people's clothes and doll clothes and evening gowns and Halloween costumes and even giant stuffed dolls with yarn hair. My doll was named Brownie with brown hair and my sister's doll was named Blondie with blonde hair. All of these treasures were tucked under the tree on Christmas morning. Nannie had a special pact with Santa Claus and somehow the gowns and dolls made their way from my Grandmother's sewing room onto Santa's sleigh.

Christmas wasn't the only holiday that set my grandmother's Singer whirling. She was also very busy in October, prior to Halloween, creating matching witch outfits for her two granddaughters. She used remnants from a large piece of black material that she had gotten for ten cents at the Woolworth store and from it she made long robes with snaps up the front. With the same material, she made capes with stand-up collars and tall pointy wide brimmed witch's hats with a mop of red yarn hair that she sewed into the inside of each hat. Add to this grotesque ensemble, a rubbery mask covered with warts and a long, crooked nose and we really looked scary. We wore our witches' outfits to our school Halloween party and won first prize for the most original costume. My grandmother was sitting in the front row with my mom, dad and Pa. Dad laughed and jokingly said that their cheers had been so loud for their two daughters, that if there had been a clap-o-meter, we would have won first prize without the judges.

Halloween

My mother loved all of the holidays and Halloween was no exception. There were bowls of candy corn and candied apples wrapped in cellophane and of course popcorn balls.

My sister and I participated in a Halloween contest at school dressed in our witch costumes that Nannie made.

Chapter Thirty-three

Always Getting into Trouble—the curse of being the oldest

I never did anything to be deliberately mischievous. I didn't wake up in the morning and say to myself, "How can I push my mother to her limit?" "How can I spend the afternoon in my room?" "How could I provoke my mother into threats of getting my father's belt or even worse, threats of tattling on me as soon as he walked in the door?"

I blame my penchants for getting on the wrong side of my mother due to the order of my birth. When you are the oldest, it is presumed that you will lead the way for your siblings. You will be a positive role model. You will do the right thing. For the most part, I really tried my darndest. However, occasionally, I made what some might consider, poor choices. Choices that were not in my best interest. Because my mother was a stay-at-home mom and Dad spent long hours at the office, most of my shenanigans had to be dealt with by my mother.

There was the time that I was walking through our neighbor's back yard. It was early winter, maybe late November, and I wanted to check on Mr. Martin's fishpond. During the summer, I would spend many hours sitting on the edge watching the giant koi navigate their wet world. With a long willow branch, I would push the giant lily pads out of the way so that I could get an unobstructed view of my Piscean friends.

But now it was winter, and I was worried. How could they possibly live if the pond was covered with a sheet of ice?

How could they breathe? How could Mr. Martin feed them? As I came closer, I could see that the edge already had a thin ridge of ice starting to form. I grabbed my stick and searched the frigid depths. There they were all huddled on the murky bottom. My worst fears confirmed. They did not look well. They hardly moved when I gently prodded them with my stick. And their color. The brilliant gold that I had so delighted in, just a month ago, was gone and had been replaced by a sickly gray hue. I was panicked and sure that if I didn't move quickly all would be lost. Mr. Martin was at work so I hustled toward home, confident that my mother would save the day. Before I reached our front door, I already had the solution. Obviously, the fish needed their gold color restored and I had seen a can of gold paint on the paint shelf in the garage. It was a simple solution. Just pour the contents of the can into the pond and voila "gold" fish. I would soon discover that there were serious flaws in my remedy. By the time I reached the pond, pried the lid off the can, and attempted to pour its contents into the water, everything came to a screeching halt. I heard screams of "No, No, No!" and spotted my mother as she raced across the backyard in my direction.

I was still in my room when my father came home from work.

Then there was the misunderstanding about some flowers that I picked for my mother. Good intentions that somehow went terribly wrong. It had been a very long winter and it had been just as long since I had wandered outside the confines of my yard. Now, it seemed that winter's cold, icy grip had finally been broken by a persistent early April and I was able to go exploring once again.

One of my favorite routes was down the bottom of the hill, behind our house, and along a thick hedgerow of evergreens that ran along the back of Miss Phillips' garden. This hedgerow formed a nearly impregnable barrier between her cherished plants and the dreaded neighborhood children. The reason that I mentioned almost impregnable is because I knew of a secret entrance that could only be accessed by crawling on one's belly through the bottom branches to the garden's edge. I found the opening and slithered to the clearing and the beginning of the garden. I was thrilled at what I saw.

Most of the snow had melted and there was an entire row of beautiful pastel crocus, all pink and yellow and purple, just inches away. All I had to do is reach out and snap them off their straw-like stems. I'd only take a few, mind you. No need to be greedy. It would make my mother so happy and Miss Phillips would never miss a couple of flowers way, way in the back of her garden. In a flash it was done, and I was tearing across the backyard grasping the ill-gotten bouquet with nary a thought of retribution.

The rest of this story is quite predictable. Mother was not at all pleased and after some intense interrogation on her part, I cracked, coming clean about where the flowers came from. Then after a good talking to, I was marched over to Miss Phillips' house, flowers in hand, to apologize for my transgression.

Once again, I was still in my room when Dad came home from the office.

Finally, there was the incident that involved Grandmother H. Mom had to make a quick run to the grocery store to pick up a few things. Her mother-in-law had arrived, unexpectedly, the night before and Mother wanted to prepare something special for dinner. She would only be gone for an hour or so and had planned on taking my sister and me with her. At the last minute, in an uncharacteristic flash of maternal bonding, our grandmother offered to watch us while Mother went on her errands. This had never happened before, and Mom was quick to show her appreciation and politely declined. Grandma H insisted and so in the end, Mother acquiesced and assured her that she was just going to the A&P and would not be long. She was also confident in the fact that we were busily playing and totally engrossed in our morning activities.

My sister and I had spent the morning pulling blankets from the linen closet to build a tent town under the dining room table and were comfortably settled in and playing cowboys and Indians. We were all decked out in full western regalia; hats, vests, boots and six shooters and ropes for lassoing uncooperative cattle. Certainly, we would need little supervision and would be preoccupied with forming a posse to track down the latest cattle rustler.

All was going well at first. My sister and I were galloping around the living room chasing the bad guy cattle rustler and our grandmother was sitting at the kitchen table reading the morning paper and enjoying a cup of hot tea.

147

Somehow that's when Grandma became the cattle rustler and we had to bring her to justice. This meant that we had to tie her up until the sheriff arrived to put her in the pokey. I sprang into action, racing around her chair, wrapping my rope around and around her. Then my sister did the same and we tied the ends of the rope into a quadruple half hitch knot in the back of her chair.

What fun! We actually had someone to capture. Mom never let us do that to her and Grandmother H seemed like she was enjoying herself. Well, at least at first. But when it was time for the Sheriff to take her off to jail, we couldn't get the knot untied and when Grandma began to struggle, the knot just got tighter and tighter.

In about a half an hour, Mom walked into the kitchen with her arms full of bags of groceries to find her husband's mother tied to a kitchen chair and her children hiding in their tent.

It wasn't long before Grandmother H headed back to Florida. Little was said about the incident and not surprisingly, it was a long time before she came to visit us again.

As I mentioned, I never intentionally wanted to upset my mother, to tick her off, to make her mad. And one must remember that there are always two sides to every stories. There was the side that Mom would tell Dad when she had had enough of my foolishness and there was my side. I was absolutely confident that everything that I told my father was the God's honest truth...to the best of my memory. He always listened very intently to my ramblings about how I really didn't mean to do anything wrong and he seemed to sympathize with me and my unfortunate circumstances. I was sure that he was on my side. And, believe me, I needed someone on my side.

Finally, there was an incident when I was in the first grade at Hendy Avenue Elementary. It must be noted that it was a trek from our house on Lovell Avenue to my school. I'm guessing probably a half mile one way. I would walk to the bottom of the hill and pick up my best friend, Irving Paltrowitz. We were in the same grade and we always walked to school together.

On one particularly cold rainy afternoon, I left my classroom and exited out the east door to meet Irving for our walk home. I had pulled my light jacket over my head to shield me from the downpour and as I got closer, I saw that Irving was motioning for me to come quickly. I hadn't noticed that his mother's car was parked by the curb. What luck! Instead of sloshing home in a torrential rainstorm, I was all comfy and warm in the back seat of Mrs. Paltrowitz's Chevy Bel Air. I sat back relishing the fact that I was being chauffeured home. It was so warm inside and so cold out that the windows were all covered with a watery mix of condensation that made it almost impossible to see out. With my hand, I wiped my window clean and that's when I spotted my mother on the sidewalk looking like a drowned rat. She was all wrapped up in her slicker, oversized boots and a plastic rain hat and was pushing my baby sister in her carriage that was completely shrouded with an old shower curtain. Mom did not look happy and as we sped by her I was only able to get off the weakest of waves to let her know that I was on my way home. Mrs. Paltrowitz dropped me off in front of my house and I scurried inside. Understandably, it must have been the last thing that my mother wanted to do that rainy afternoon. The baby carriage had to be pulled out of the garage, my sister had to be wrapped in a heavy jacket and a ton of blankets, Mom had to find her boots in the back of the coat closet, and then trudge through the pouring rain to pick me up from school. I must admit that I was caught off guard by just how angry Mom was when she finally got home. She was livid. In my defense, this was the first time ever—ever—that my mother had come to school to pick me up. What was I supposed to do? Ask Irving's mother to stop the car?

I'm sorry to report that, my explanation of events fell on deaf ears. There would be no waiting for my father to come home. The trial was over. The judge had reached her verdict. I was found guilty and there would be no appeal, no clemency. The sentence was one week of being grounded. I had to go directly to my room after school and no trips to Nannie's house on the weekend.

I was ordered to my room to think about what I had done. This might take a while.

Chapter Thirty-four
The Beginnings of a Power Couple—eat, drink and make connections

We continued to spend our summers at the cottage with Dad commuting and Mom and Nannie busy doing what they loved. There was an abundance of strawberries and grapes that were made into jams and jellies and homemade root beer that was stirred in a big pot before being poured into corked bottles and stored away for fermentation. Recipes were clipped from the latest edition of the Ladies Home Journal and pasted into scrapbooks. Pa, retired now, spent his days snoozing, in a big rocker, on the front porch. My grandfather, also, had a comfy overstuffed chair in the living room, right next to the radio, so that he would never miss a *broadcast of a Brooklyn Dodgers baseball game.*

The weekends were filled with card games and fishing and collecting wild blackberries in the woods behind the house. There was also a steady stream of extended family members and friends from my parents' ever-expanding social circle and Dad's business buddies. Interestingly enough, the extended family was a short list of my father's aunts, Kathleen and Betty and Mom's sister. Conspicuously absent was any sign of a cousin. "No cousins? That's weird" was always the reaction of my friends. I mentioned before that there was a preponderance of only children in our family, hence, no cousins.

Grandma H had two sisters, one was a spinster and the other married late in life and was childless. And my father was an only child. On Mom's side, her parents, Nannie and

Pa were both only children. They had two kids, my aunt who never had children and Mom. The consequence of a family with so little procreation, was a family without cousins. But remember the old saying, "You don't miss what you don't have" most certainly rang true for me. To be honest, I was relieved that I didn't have any cousins that I would have to share my Nannie with. It was bad enough that I had to share her with my sister.

There was certainly no scarcity of friends. There were friends of my parents and friends of mine. Dad was more than obliging when asked to pick up one of my school chums to spend the weekend at the lake. Arrangements between the moms would be made in advance and my father would pick up my friend when he left his office. Of course, I never dared to mention inviting Irving Paltrowitz. I knew that a boy would not be coming for a sleep over, even if he was my best friend. Mom's old nursing buddies and their spouses, Dad's business associates, and friends from the country club, and their neighbors on Lovell Avenue were all too eager to accept an invitation that was certain to be worth the long drive. My parents were becoming quite the popular power couple. They had it all. They were good looking, good natured, incredibly social and loved entertaining albeit a small dinner party, cocktails and hors d'oeuvres for a crowd or a buffet brunch on Sunday morning. Mom and Dad were in their element.

Entertaining at the lake was made easier with my grandmother sharing the culinary challenges, of which there were many. Mother was never one to take the easy path.

When she put on a party, she put on a party. Forget the chip and dip and bowls of Planter's peanuts. A cocktail party involved two very important elements. Cocktails and food.

Cocktails during the nineteen fifties were potent potables that, after tipping back a few, would most assuredly loosen up even the staidest of guests. Manhattans made with Seagram's whiskey, sweet vermouth and just a splash of maraschino cherry juice…Martinis made with Beefeater's gin and a whisper of dry vermouth…Old fashions, a concoction of Kentucky bourbon, muddled citrus and sugar, Angostura bitters, topped off with a fizzy bit of club soda. These were their secret weapons to a successful shindig. The trilogy. The trifecta.

Not to be overlooked were highballs, rye, scotch or bourbon with club soda or lowballs, with the aforementioned whiskeys either on the rocks or neat. On the rare occasion, when the lake breeze was conspicuously absent, Mom would shift to gin and tonic (served in tall, slender, pastel frosted glasses) with a wheel of lime hitched to the rim of the glass or a large pitcher of lemony rum daiquiris or maybe a "not for children" fruit punch. There was never wine nor beer served at my mother's cocktail parties. Wine was for drinking during dinner and beer was relegated to a Styrofoam cooler on a picnic or plastic cup at a sports event.

Drinks were important but a party wouldn't be a party without an abundance of delicious hors d'oeuvres. Finger foods on a cocktail napkin that a guest could, with some practice, learn to balance in one hand with a drink in the other. All of this had to be carried out sans table or chair while roaming around carrying on multiple conversations with a gazillion different people. Sort of like rubbing your stomach and patting your head at the same time. When done properly on the professional cocktail circuit, it was fascinating to watch.

There was a rule in our house that if we were quiet (Dad would say "Make yourself scarce") we could hang around. My sister and I would find an inconspicuous little cubbyhole, with a good vantage point to curl up in and be vicariously part of all the adultness. Mom already had us in our pajamas, teeth brushed and hair combed so that if we did not follow the rules, it took only a stern glance towards our bedroom to know that the party was over for us.

Food preparation for a typical cocktail party took on marathon proportions and several days of extensive preparation. Nannie would scrub yellow peppers, celery, cauliflower and radishes for the crudité and whip up yummy blue cheese sauce for dipping. Using a potato peeler, Mother would make carrot curls. Long strips of carrot that she would roll up like a pin curl, held together with a toothpick and kept in a bowl of ice water in the fridge until ready to serve. Nannie brought jars of pickles, sweet little gherkins and watermelon rind from Herrick Street and cut-glass relish platters, bowls and special serving trays. The copper chafing dishes had to be washed and polished and made ready for the Swedish meatballs. There was asparagus and green beans to steam and eggs to boil for Nannie's famously delicious deviled eggs and shrimp to boil, peel and clean for shrimp cocktail. Mom made a killer cocktail sauce with catsup, lemon juice and enough horseradish to curl your hair.

But the real crowd pleaser, the piece de resistance, were my mother's rolled sandwiches. These were delicate spirals, just pop one in your mouth, delicious! The bread was ordered specially sliced long ways from the bakery. An average loaf would yield four maybe five long rectangular pieces. Then using a rolling pin, each piece was rolled paper thin and softened butter was spread from edge to edge. My grandmother made yummy egg salad with just a whisper of Frenches mustard, ham salad with finely chopped pickle, and last and probably my least favorite, pimento, chopped green olives and cream cheese filling.

I groused about the latter to no avail. Mother always made the same number of each, six egg salad rolled sandwiches (when the sandwiches were sliced, each would yield about five or six delectable orbs) six ham salad and six cream cheese and pimento. In that exact order, they would disappear from Nannie's fancy serving trays. I questioned my mother on many an occasion to ask why we even had to make those silly olive ones and her reply was always the same "Because that's the way it's always been." I guess that's good enough for me, likeI really have a vote in this election. I have my own theory. You see, I think that Mom liked the cream cheese and pimento best and knew that even when the party was over and she finally had a moment to sit down and kick off her high heels, she could curl up with a lovely chilled Manhattan and with cocktail napkin stacked high with you guessed it. Pimento and cream cheese rolled sandwiches. My mother was no fool.

And so they came. They came to drink. They came to eat. They came to gossip and talk shop. They came to socialize, to make connections, to do business and maybe even some occasional monkey business. They were insurance men like my dad and doctors and nurses, friends of my mothers. There were lawyers and accountants from Perry and Maxy and they all had much in common. They were young and ambitious, smart and hardworking, babies of the Great Depression, whose parents had struggled with the total collapse of the U.S. economy. As difficult as things had been, somehow this generation, unlike their parents, had been insulated from the all too real hardship of surviving the horrific nightmare of financial catastrophe. What followed was World War II and prosperity. The prosperity train that my parents intended to ride to a future full of rainbows. Success and financial security for their children and for their parents that had sacrificed so much.

The word spread about this popular young couple and their penchants for entertaining. Even their neighbors on the lake wanted in on the revelry. One in particular, a dentist who lived in a lovely old log house on the north side, had become quite chummy with my father and had all but invited himself to a cocktail party one particular Saturday night. After the crowd had made their way back up the twisty lake road toward civilization and after probably one too many rye and sodas, my father and his new acquaintance found themselves sitting at the old picnic table in the side yard talking about what ever one talks about after too many cocktails. Old lovers, lost lovers, deals that went sour, politics and life...what they wanted...what they needed...expectations and goals, et cetera, et cetera.

Not long after their first meeting, my Dad's dentist friend from next door phoned with some very interesting news. It just so happened that his insurance agent in Watkins Glen, the tiny hamlet at the bottom of the lake, was intent on retiring and wanted to sell his agency. He and his wife were planning on pulling up stakes and heading to the west coast of Florida, which meant that he would not only be selling his business but his house as well. This is where things got very interesting. The house was a beautiful old Victorian mansion built in 1890. It clung to a hillside looking down on the town, perfectly juxtaposed between the business district and neat little rows of much more modest houses. He assured my father that this was a must-see and a must-see right away, before it was listed with a realtor or possibly scooped up before it even hit the market. This might very well be a chance of a lifetime and one that Dad was not going to let slip through his fingers.

Chapter Thirty-five

Seeing Fourth Street for The First Time—big house, big plans

We pulled up in front of the house at nine o'clock sharp the following Saturday morning. Dad was dressed in a gray shark skin suit with a cobalt blue striped tie (the blue stripe was a perfect match for his Paul Newman eyes) and black cashmere topcoat. He certainly looked the part...business owner, squire of a village manor, a big fish ready to swim in the little pond.

Mother was looking her loveliest. Perfectly coiffed, her chestnut hair brushed in a stylish pageboy. She was perfectly made up. Red lips, mascara and most certainly not a bit of shine on her nose. Stockings, high heels, white gloves and a lovely wool tweed wrap coat with a beaver collar. They were stunning.

We were given our orders to exit the back seat of the car and I was to hold Dad's hand and my sister would hold Mom's. We were not to let go for any reason. Even if the nice people who were showing us the house said. "The children are more than welcome to explore. No need for them to be shackled to their parents." Not even if Dad accidently let go of my hand in his preoccupation of looking at something. I was to stick like glue. No excuses, no exceptions. Don't touch anything, don't sit down on the furniture and don't pick up a tchotchke. And for heaven sakes, keep your hands away from your face or to be more precise, your nose. Finally, be quiet, very, very quiet. Not a word, not a peep. As quiet as little mice, as mother liked to say.

As we approached the front porch, the giant hand carved wooden doors swung open and we were welcomed into the hallway that led into the insurance office. Two grand mahogany desks sat side by side. Behind the first one was perched a tiny bespectacled secretary pounding away at a typewriter, stacks and stacks of envelopes and policies towering above her. The second desk was covered with even more official documents, seemingly waiting to be scrutinized and signed. There was a gilded name plate with a gold ballpoint pen, on the front of the desk, for the tasks at hand. Against the back wall, next to the fireplace, was a huge safe with its door flung open and four rather uncomfortable looking chairs, to accommodate the customers, sat in front of the desks.

From there, we entered the main part of the house. Huge rooms, tall ceilings, tons of elaborate casing around the doorways, beautiful hardwood floors, floor to ceiling windows and fireplaces. There was a fireplace in almost every room. Who ever heard of such an extravagance? The kitchen was enormous, almost as big as our entire downstairs on Lovell Avenue. And pink, cotton candy pink. I had never seen a pink kitchen before. Upstairs was more of the same. More tall ceilings, more lovely floors, tall windows, ornate woodwork and big, very, very big. It was scary big.

It turned out that my parents didn't have a bit of a worry about us running off and causing some kind of a ruckus. That was the furthest thing from my mind. To be perfectly honest, I couldn't have been pried loose from my father's hand. A child lost in this house would be lost forever. Destined to grow old and gray roaming the empty halls. I was absolutely terrified by the prospect of being separated from my parents, of being left behind, gawking out of an upstairs window as I watched our station wagon disappear into nothingness.

That night was filled with dreams of darting through unfamiliar hallways, dimly lit with closed doors that led to the same. Windowless corridors draped with ancient tapestries and portraits of stone-faced strangers who leered down at me as I begged them for even the tiniest clue of an escape route. But their lips sat motionless on the canvas. Only their eyes swiveled back and forth, giving them all a creepy owl-like appearance. I scurried through the labyrinth of empty rooms; a mouse trapped in an unforgiving maze. Turning left and right in a frenzy of futility. But to no avail. It became clear that the only way that I could be rescued would be to let out a blood curdling scream. Maybe not a scream that would wake the dead but definitely one that would wake my parents.

Chapter Thirty-six

The Move—the beginning of a new life

Mother promised that she would take me to town to pick out a present for my teacher. Friday would be my last day at Hendy Avenue and I wanted to impress my teacher with something more than a box of Whitman's chocolates. After wandering up and down the aisles of Woolworth's and not finding the perfect gift, I dragged Mom down the street to Iszard's hoping for a better selection. We rummaged through boxes of monogramed stationary, gold chains and black and white bangle bracelets, lace hankies with a delicate E (her last name was Eliott) embroidered on their corners, and bottles of toilet water that we sprayed with abandon.

Now Mother had been a good sport, a real trooper, but I realized that the clock was ticking, and my options were quickly running out. There was one last aisle to explore and I was sure that I'd find what I was looking for. As we turned the corner, to my amazement, there it was. A beautiful, cream colored porcelain statue of a wild stallion. A magnificent stallion, rearing on his haunches, all gold and glittering. I knew for a fact that Mrs. Eliott was as crazy for horses as I was. It was the perfect gift.

The Tri City Moving Company

Call us at RE-22923 for all your moving needs

"Trust us with your stuff!"

DEPENDABLE & RELIABLE

This was scrawled on the side of the huge truck that was parked right in front of our house on Lovell Avenue. I wasn't at all sure that I wanted to trust these total strangers with my stuff, but Dad assured me that they were, indeed, dependable and reliable. My father promised me that they would very carefully pack up all my toys and dolls and books and clothes and even my cowgirl stuff.

Everything was wrapped in brown butcher paper and packed in boxes for the hour ride to their new home. By midafternoon, the moving van was bulging with our belongings. The rear doors were slammed closed and secured by a metal bar.

The four burly moving men squished into the cab as the driver revved the motor and black exhaust heaved out of the tailpipe. They were ready to go. And so were we. The station wagon, a microcosm of its larger counterpart, was stuffed to overflowing with people and possessions, all rumbling down route 14 heading north with Nannie and Pa bringing up the rear.

Mother was the designated drill sergeant, in command of her post at the front door, barking directives as everything was carried into the house. Motioning boxes of cookbooks, pots and pans and dishes, silverware and fine china, dish towels and canned goods to the kitchen where Nannie stood at the ready to get everything tucked away in the cupboards.

A pair of wingback chairs cozied up to one of the fireplaces. The oversized couch fit perfectly in front of the bay windows with plenty of room for matching lamps that were perched atop twin mahogany end tables.

Beds and dressers and all things bedroom were maneuvered up the winding staircase and Dad met them with a screwdriver in hand. Mom always wanted the beds to be put together straight away so that fresh sheets, pillows and blankets could ready each bed for the long awaited first night in their new home.

Grandmother H's formal dining room furniture marched down the narrow hallway to the dining room. The pieces that had seemed so huge in our house in Elmira were now dwarfed in this massive room that would soon be hosting family holiday meals, birthday parties, Sunday afternoon dinners with Nannie and Pa and parties, cocktail parties and dinner parties. Lots and lots of parties.

It didn't take long for us to make Fourth Street our home. The rooms that had seemed so cavernous on my first visit soon became my new normal. How silly I had been to worry about losing my way, about being separated from my parents.

On the second day in the house, Nannie and I had worked all morning getting all my prized possessions unpacked and put away. Pa had put up three rows of wooden shelves next to my dresser and Mother had promised to paint everything lavender as soon as she got a minute. In the meantime, I filled the shelves with my most favorite things. On the lowest shelf, that I could easily reach, I stacked all my much-read books and there were a ton of them. Titles such as "Millions of Cats", "Little Black Sambo", "The Wind in the Willows", books of English fairy tales and poems by Robert Louis Stevenson and Lewis Carroll.

The second shelf was the perfect place for my ceramic horse collection that was growing exponentially on every birthday and wrapped in gold tissue paper in my Christmas stocking. At last count there were twelve and they were beauties. One was a replica of Gene Autry's horse, Champion, while another was Roy Roger's palomino, Trigger. There was a figurine that I had gotten from a friend on my birthday that looked just like one of the horses on the merry-go-round at Eldridge Park. It was painted with brilliant rainbow colors and its golden mane and tail were outstretched like a flag on a windy day. The top shelf remained empty for the time being, which was a good thing, because Nannie couldn't reach up there even if she stood on tippy toes.

My dresser and closet filled up quickly. Dresses, coats, sweaters, skirts and blouses all went on hangers while undies, shirts, pants, shorts, pajamas were all neatly folded in their assigned drawer. Socks (and I had a ton of them) were rolled into perfect balls and lived in a drawer of their own.

On Wednesday, Nannie and Pa said their goodbyes and tootled back to Herrick Street. I only let her go after she promised to come back on Sunday afternoon for dinner. I purposely took refuge in my room while the rest of the family walked them to their car. From my vantage point, crouched on the floor next to a window, I could hear my parents laughing and happily talking as they waved goodbye. I was able to catch just a glimpse of Nannie's blue Oldsmobile as it headed down the hill. A resolute sense of abandonment swept over me as I crumbled into a wet ball of tears. What was the matter with my parents? How could they be so happy when Nannie and Pa were leaving? How was I ever going to survive until Sunday afternoon?

On the fateful day of their return, I perched myself on a dining room chair that I had dragged over to a window. It was the perfect spot for monitoring the comings of any car up the Decatur Street hill. At last, the Sunday that seemed to have taken months to arrive, was here.

My requests for the approximate time of my grandparent's arrival had been largely ignored as Mother scurried around the kitchen. She reminded me of a mad maestro, spatula waving over her orchestra of pots and pans, all bubbling in perfect harmony on the stove.

I was going to try to be vigilant. I was going to try to be patient. Maybe it would help if I made up a game, like counting all the cars that passed by. That didn't work. By the time I got to twenty-four or was it twenty-five, I had lost count. It might be more fun to keep track of the different colors of cars. When I had counted four white, two black, and a yellow station wagon with wood panels on the sides, there it was, the blue car that I had been waiting for.

I totally ignored my mother's request that I put on a coat and hat and shot out of the side door and up the steps. Pa was unpacking the car and Nannie was supervising the transport of dishes that she had prepared for Sunday dinner. She was particularly concerned about his handling of the pie carrier and the possible destruction of her treasured meringue. By some miracle and repeated trips up and down and back and forth, everything made it to the kitchen without incident. There were scalloped potatoes that Nannie had wrapped in an old dish towel. There were pies, one cherry, one apple and one coconut cream with its waves of meringue. There was a baked ham smeared with a brown sugar glaze, dotted with fragrant cloves and rings of pineapple.

Mother had roasted a chicken, steamed some Brussel sprouts and made her signature poppy seed studded dinner rolls. The table was set with Mother's Candlewick and Grandma H's sterling silver. There was the old family linen tablecloth and matching napkins, all meticulously ironed and everyone had a fancy water glass, even my sister and me. Two platters took their positions of importance in the center of the table. One for the ham and one for the chicken. Six chairs placed strategically in front of the six place settings were ready for our first family dinner in our new home.

When Mother called to let us know that the food was on the table, we all hustled into the dining room and began circling the table like some crazy game of musical chairs. On Lovell Avenue, we knew exactly where everyone sat and at Nannie's house, we knew exactly where everyone sat but here on Fourth Street, it was a whole new ball game. Thank goodness, Mother stepped in and assigned seats. My father was at the head of the table, of course, Nannie and Pa sat together on the left side, my sister and I sat across from them and Mom sat at the other end of the table, closest to the kitchen, so she could make a quick exit to fetch whatever she might have forgotten. Extra gravy, more potatoes, the salt shaker, the pepper shaker, a clean spoon for my sister who was forever dropping hers on the floor, and not to be forgotten, dessert. In this case pie.

Chapter Thirty-seven

Adjusting to Their New Surroundings—new town, new business

Dad had no problem taking over the reins of his newly acquired insurance business. Sitting in his oversized leather office chair, he looked the part, he looked confident, he looked business like, he looked handsome. He seemed to relish life in a small town, traipsing down the street or popping into the stores, introducing himself, shaking hands and making small talk, making connections, making friends.

He joined the Rotary Club, the Chamber of Commerce, the Elks Club, he was a Mason, and started to dabble a bit in local politics. Business was done over a cup of coffee at Chef's Diner or at the Elks Club, after a couple of cocktails and a friendly game of gin rummy. Business was good.

A metal sign hung from our front porch, J.R. Havens Insurance Agency. A sign that could be easily seen from the sometimes sleepy and sometimes bustling little village below.

Mother had taken a hiatus from nursing and decided to help my dad in the office. It was perfect timing as my sister and I were starting classes at our new school, and how convenient was it, having the office in the house. After she got us off to school, washed the breakfast dishes and made the beds, it was off with the apron and on with business attire. A quick brush of her hair and some lips and she was all set. It was no more than a half dozen steps from our living quarters to the office. A desk was added to the others, close to the large bay window.

Mother was in charge of everything that her husband wasn't so good at. Number one being paperwork. My father made any excuse to avoid paperwork and my mother, being a typical type A personality, was all about being organized, being on top of things. It was a business match made in heaven. Dad sold the policies and Mother, under the tutelage of the agency's long-time secretary, did the rest. There was plenty of work for them both; lots of typing, getting with the underwriter, figuring the cost and most importantly, collecting the premiums.

Dad absolutely hated the money part and would go to great lengths to avoid any such conversation. He was notorious for excusing himself, ever so politely, with every indication that he would be right back and be seen scurrying out the kitchen door, making a mad dash to his car and speeding away to the relative sanctity of one of the many male only bastions about town. There was the Elks Club for a quick card game or the Jefferson Hotel for a quick cocktail or even a quick cup of coffee at Chef's Diner. After all, he was just taking care of business, making connections, schmoozing all in the name of business.

So yes, life was good for my father. He had found his niche, a business that he enjoyed and one that provided a very comfortable lifestyle for his wife and daughters, a stately old Victorian jewel that was admired by many a town's person and a lovely little village, so picturesque and familiar that it could have leapt off a Norman Rockwell canvas.

Mother was enjoying her new assignment. Her presence in the office gave the business an air of efficiency and competence. A quick study, she made her transformation from medicine to insurance appear seamless. She became a fixture in the office, setting up shop at the desk next to the window that gave her a view of the Fourth Street hill.

Customers were greeted by either my mother or Dad's secretary, Jennie, who as I mentioned, had worked at the agency for many years and knew everyone. Though knowing everyone might seem like a daunting task. It was actually not that big of a deal when one realized, that in a village with a population of twelve hundred, everyone knows everyone. That can be a good thing or a not so good thing. It meant that you either had many acquaintances, all very interested in you and everything that you did or that some folks were always in your business. It's a matter of personal perception, your need for anonymity or your willingness to relinquish some privacy. My parents were more than willing to embrace a less private lifestyle, for the social and business advantages that this small town offered.

Chapter Thirty-eight

You Promised Us a Dog—my parents are called to task

Bribery, to be terribly blunt, has for generations been the indispensable tool of mothers and fathers, who needed just a bit of leverage when trying to persuade their children to accept something new, something different.

When my parents casually floated the idea of a dog being part of the "wouldn't it be fun to move" discussion, the dog word stuck in my brain like an all-day sucker. I couldn't imagine that my mother and father would be foolish enough to think that their firstborn was going to forget about that.

It had been a year since I lost my dog Jip and it was high time that I had another canine in my life. For a change, Mother was the easy sell and Dad was the naysayer.

Mom had grown up with dogs, she was crazy about dogs. She was, most assuredly, a dog person. Her constant companion when she was a teenager was a beautiful snow-white German Shephard named Dawnie. And before Dawnie there was a long line of canine predecessors, all large formidable beasts that occupied a place of prominence on my grandparent's front porch on Herrick Street.

It only made sense that I should first approach my mother with a gentle reminder of the dog promise. Timing was crucial. School was over at two-thirty and it took me about twenty minutes to trudge up the hill to our house. Mother usually left the office around three-thirty, made my sister and me a snack and started dinner preparation. Dad would be home around four-thirty and dinner was on the table at five o'clock sharp. Following her mother's tradition, this was the same time that dinner was always served on Herrick Street.

This was my window. After I gobbled down my peanut butter and jelly sandwich and polished off a glass of milk, I nonchalantly mentioned the "D" word. Mother didn't seem to skip a beat—or a chop to be more precise—at the mention of a pet. It was only later that I realized that she had a plan. Dad was not a dog lover. Unlike Mom, he had not been allowed to have pets when he was a child. Grandmother H. didn't see the value of a fuzzy friend. She thought that a dog was nothing more than a stinky nuisance that would shed hair on her Persian rugs and pee on her sacred hydrangea bushes.

Our plan of attack called for a strategic, well-thought out approach. We had to be clever and cunning if we were going to pull the wool over my father's eyes. Mother thought that possibly, a diversion might work. Her husband had to be convinced that this was the perfect time for a doggie addition to our family. However, before any negotiations could begin, Mom demanded that if, indeed, we got a dog, I would be in-charge of the day to day maintenance of the animal. I swore that I would feed the dog and brush the dog and walk the dog and clean up its poop. I hoped that Mom didn't see my fingers crossed behind my back when I made this pledge.

Paramount to our argument was the fulfillment of my parents' promise. What about their promise? New house, new dog. Then there was the matter of security. A dog would protect us from any stranger breaking into our house. Except for the fact that there were no strangers in our tiny town and zero crime. A moot point, in my opinion.

It had been decided that a cat for Dad would be our secret weapon. My father loved cats. Big, small, skinny, fat, striped or tabby, he loved them all. This was the old bait and switch trick or your classic quid pro quo. We would find a cute, little fluffy kitten for Dad and then when he least expected it, we would spring the dog idea on him. He wouldn't be able to say no. It was the perfect plan. First thing in the morning, Mother would start her search.

There was one person in our town that knew absolutely everything that was going on at any given second. Her name was Patty Francis and she was the town's only telephone operator. Whenever you wanted to call someone, you simply picked up the receiver and told Patty who you wanted to speak to. In addition to that, you might want to know if the A&P had ground beef on sale, or if Helen Fraboni was going to Florida for the winter, or if the new dentist in town was any good, or in this case, did she know of anyone who might have a kitten for sale?

As it turned out, Alice Williams, who lived on Decatur Street, had just put an ad in the Watkins Review offering free kittens to a good home. With the push and pull of a couple of plugs, cords and switches, Mother was talking to Mrs. Williams and arranged a time to come and take a look.

I had begged her to wait until I got home from school so that I could tag along. Mom agreed, as long as I came directly home.

In class the next day, I watched the giant clock over the blackboard as the minute hand crawled toward the six. At last, the bell rang and jolted me out of my seat. I grabbed my coat and didn't waste a minute before rushing out the door. No, indeed, there would be no dillydallying today.

Mrs. Williams greeted us at the front door and we followed her to the laundry room, in the back of the house, where mother cat was curled up with her babies. An old blanket that had been laid next to the washing machine provided a cozy nest for the newly born and the mother cat.

Understandably, mother cat didn't seem at all excited to see us. As a matter of fact, we were alerted to her displeasure with a strange guttural growl that morphed into a long, spitty hiss. She was giving us fair warning that we were not welcome.

Thankfully, mother noticed two little outliers rolled up in one corner of the blanket and we cautiously approached, one eye on the kittens and one eye on the mother. Mrs. Williams bent over the two tiny balls of fluff and gently scooped them up and wrapped them in her apron for our inspection. They were both females. One was black and gray and the other was orange and white. Mother cat was a domestic long hair so we had a pretty good idea of what these babies would look like when they grew up. They were adorable. Dad would not be able to resist. Although we had not planned on two kittens, they seemed so close and comfortable with each other, that Mom just didn't have the heart to separate them. It was already too late for me. I was smitten. I was in love with them both. I had bonded. We would come back in four weeks when they were a bit older and take them home.

The timing was perfect. April fifth was my father's birthday and now we had the perfect birthday present. Mother had left the office early that day to get everything ready for the celebration and Nannie and Pa were to arrive around four o'clock.

My job was to blow up balloons, set the table and make Dad a birthday card. Birthday cards were my specialty. I spread the contents of the huge plastic container of art supplies out on the kitchen table and began to sift through everything to find what I needed. Blue construction paper (blue was his favorite color) red paper for hearts, scissors, glue and my giant box of Crayola crayons, the one with gold and silver and copper and burnt umber. The one that Nannie, oh no, I mean Santa Claus had gotten me for Christmas.

Mother had a chocolate cake in the oven and seven-minute icing was bubbling in a double boiler on the stove. Dad had requested some of Nannie's famous Swiss steak that was in route, wrapped in an old bath towel, on the back seat of my grandparent's Oldsmobile.

The kittens were all cozy in a cardboard box tucked next to the furnace in the basement.

The party was a huge success. We chatted and chewed, chewed and chatted. Dinner was delicious. We sang happy birthday and laughed and gobbled down dessert, all in anticipation of the opening of presents.

Dad tore off wrapping paper, opened boxes and then ceremoniously displayed his bounty. There was a navy-blue polka dotted necktie, a bottle of Seagram's Seven and a coffee mug inscribed with "The World's Best Dad".

Mother had slipped out of the dining room and headed to the cellar to retrieve the grand prize. She quickly closed the flaps of the box, leaving a crack in the top for air. After reassuring our newest family members that everything would be just fine, she tied a large strip of blue satin ribbon around the box and made her way back to the dining room for the grand reveal. I tried my best to be nonchalant, pretending that I had no idea of what could possibly be in the box, but I failed miserably. By the time the present of all presents had been placed in front of the birthday boy, I had totally lost control. I jumped out of my chair and positioned myself next to Dad in case he needed my assistance getting the ribbon off. The entire time, I was bouncing up and down and begging him to hurry. When he opened the lid, he was greeted by the mews of his very own kitties and he was delighted. He pulled them out by the scruffs of their necks and cradled them in his lap so that he could take a better look. Yes, this was the perfect present for my father. This was the best birthday party ever!

The kittens grew quickly. Dad named the black and gray one Miss Boots and her sister Trixie. Soon, they were scampering everywhere and making themselves comfortable in their new digs. They learned to negotiate the circular staircase and navigate the maze of rooms, both upstairs and down, staking out their territory and securing their secret hiding places when they were not in the mood for human contact. Of course, they always magically appeared when Dad got home and rattled their dishes announcing that dinner was served.

On one particular night, only Miss Boots showed up for dinner. We were all sent out on a reconnaissance mission. We spread out. Mom took the downstairs. Dad checked outside and my sister and I were assigned to the bedrooms upstairs. We looked under all the beds, behind the dressers, and crawled into the back of all the closets, but Trixie was nowhere to be found. Her name echoed through the house as we called her over and over again. But no Trixie. Mother searched behind all the furniture in the living room, on top of the china cabinet and even in the fireplaces. But no Trixie. Dad called her name as he walked along the hedge row on the north side of our property, under the cars that were parked on the street and the front porch where she could often be found snoozing on an old wicker chair. But no Trixie. It wasn't until the next morning that Dad finally found her under the lilac bush in the side yard. He got a shovel from the basement and buried her quickly. I found a rock in Mom's garden and painted her name on it, encircled with flowers. We fashioned a cross out of two sticks and some scotch tape to make a marker for her grave. My sister and I had our own private graveyard service. We picked some flowers and pushed them into the ground next to the cross and said our goodbyes.

Chapter Thirty-nine

A Village like So Many—and yet so much more

During the Ice Age, rivers of frozen water scraped through the unforgiving bedrock of what thousands of years later, I would call home. In the 1800's, commerce and the availability of transportation, via lakes, gave rise to a proliferation of tiny towns that grew like swamp grass on the water's edge. These towns provided homes for the workers and their families who followed industry with the expressed desire to fulfill their perception of the American dream. Watkins Glen was just such a town, though a tiny dot on the Atlas road map, it was the County Seat, home to the fledgling Formula I Grand Prix road race, and Watkins Glen State Park.

Watkins Glen State Park, or to be more precise, the Glen was a huge tourist attraction. Its presence so obvious, such a marvel of Mother Nature that the village could hardly avoid being named in its honor. Tourists flocked there by the thousands. They parked their cars at the lower entrance and trudged up hundreds of stone steps, ducked behind waterfalls that cascaded over the narrow rock pathways, and stopped to rest at the water's edge, perched on a wall of shale. Some had said that its beauty was so remarkable that it should be considered the eighth wonder of the world.

It has been noted that, when you live near such a tourist attraction as the Glen, one seldom goes there, and we had never been there. It's sort of like living near the ocean and the only time you go there is when relatives come to visit.

Or if you live in New York City and you've never been to the top of the Empire State Building. And to make matters worse, practically every day we drove by the entrance to the Glen and from my vantage point in the back seat of the station wagon, I would only catch a glimpse of the rocks and water and people. Flying by at forty miles an hour wasn't what I had in mind.

One night after dinner, while Mom was busy clearing the table and Dad was finishing his bowl of rice pudding, I realized that it might be the perfect time to mention that we had lived in our house for almost six months and we hadn't even been to the Glen. I was fully prepared for rebuttal. It was supposed to be a beautiful weekend, perfect weather, and the trip to the top only took a couple of hours. We would be home in plenty of time for Dad's baseball game. A friend at school had told me that you could take a taxi to the top and then make the much easier trek down. To my amazement, there was no need for any of this. They both nodded their heads in agreement and confirmed that a trip to the Glen would be great fun. Yes, we were all going to hike up the Glen on Saturday morning. I couldn't wait.

The Glen was beautiful, without a doubt. Everywhere I looked it was wet and shiny black, with jagged chards of sedimentary rock and pools with foamy torrents of swirling water and mossy green cliffs that were proof that plants could grow in the most unlikely places. At times, the roar of cascading water was deafening, as it poured over the rocky cliffs. Just as quickly, everything changed. Raging water relaxed into limpid pools devoid of the slightest movement and there was a silence that one might only experience in nature.

We finally made it to the top where there was a stone bench waiting for my weary parents. But it was a row of well-worn swings, dangling from their rusty chains, and a pair of wooden see saws that attracted my attention. "Watch me! Watch me!" I bellowed as I pumped my toothpick legs with the determination of a marathon runner. Watch me! Watch me! But they paid absolutely no attention to my warbling. What could be so important? Why were they so preoccupied, so engrossed in conversation? This was definitely grown-up talk. It was evident that Mother was not going to be able to make the trek back down the one thousand four hundred and seventy-six steps to the parking lot and our awaiting car. Dad had scurried off only to return minutes later with the taxi driver who was parked next to the concession stand. The next thing I knew, we were all stuffed into the backseat of the cab headed toward the lower entrance. I knew better than to ask too many questions at a time like this and was content to simply stare out the window at the blur of evergreens, as we sped down the hill.

What could possibly be the matter?

Chapter Forty
The Family Grows—a baby brother

The nineteen fifties was not a decade of enlightenment for children. At least not in this family. Words like menstruation, breasts, or God forbid, pregnancy were never mentioned. A baby was delivered to your house in a diaper sling via a large white bird with a yellow beak. And I'm assuming that's how I got my brother. He arrived in early January and I was delighted.

I saw no reason why Mother should have to spend all her time with the baby when I was not in school. She was a busy woman working in Dad's office, cooking, cleaning, doing the washing and ironing and a gazillion other things. I was more than willing to pitch in with diaper changes and bottles of formula and rocking and taking him out on the porch for a breath of fresh air. Nannie would say to "Get the stink blow'd off".

I was the older sister, after all, and even before the baby came, I was negotiating for my rights of access. Foremost, on my list of demands was that I wanted the baby to sleep in my room on his first night home from the hospital and every night thereafter. Maybe Mom was busy giving my sister a bath. Maybe it was all that splashing of water in the tub. Maybe it was all that high-pitched squealing from my little sister as all of the bubbles were rinsed from her soapy head. I don't know exactly what it was but after an unrelenting tirade of incessant begging and pleading, she actually agreed to my ridiculous demand. I even made her cross her heart and swear to God. The deal was sealed!

"Now please go play and leave me alone." I'm sure that she thought that in three months I would have totally forgotten about her promise, but she was so mistaken.

Mom's tummy got bigger and bigger (typically, there was never any mention of a pregnancy). The bassinet was pulled out of the attic and given yet another fresh coat of white paint and then took its place in a corner of my parent's bedroom. There was a tiny blue dresser and a changing table that was piled high with a cloud of pearly white diapers, undershirts that snapped on the side, nightgowns with drawstring bottoms and booties that were knitted by one of the ladies in Nannie's sewing circle. There was Johnson's baby powder to sprinkle on his bottom and a gooey white cream that was to be generously applied at the slightest sign of a diaper rash. Cotton swabs and cotton balls and diaper pins and a box of tissues for the messy jobs. All seemed ready.

So, I wasn't terribly surprised when one morning in early January, I trudged downstairs for breakfast and found my grandmother busily frying up some bacon and poaching eggs for my sister and me. Mother and Dad had left around three AM and had passed the childcare baton to my grandparents as they scurried up the hill to the car. Nannie and Pa would be staying with us for several weeks to help Mom recuperate and make sure that the baby was on a good schedule.

A good schedule had everything to do with how often the baby was fed. Ideally, it was a bottle of formula every four hours and this regiment was religiously adhered to. This was only accomplished if the baby cooperated and there lies the rub. That's why a rocking chair was a must have piece of furniture. You had to have a rocking chair. A rocking chair in the living room and a rocking chair upstairs in the bedroom and we had both. There was no question that this baby was going to be doing some serious rocking.

There was one tiny little problem and that had to do with the location of my brother's bassinet. It was not in my room as had been promised. This was something that I had to talk to my grandmother about right away. I told her the entire story...mother had told me that I would be able to sleep with the new baby as soon as he came home from the hospital. Consequently, when I got home from school, I would be moving my brother's bed into my room. Nannie had, with all the patience of Job, listened to me go on and on. When I had exhausted all avenues of logic, she looked up from whatever she was doing and scolded, "Hold your horses, young lady. I'll be speaking to your mother about that." I couldn't help interjecting, "But Nannie, crisscross my heart. Mom promised. I'm not telling a lie. She promised."

As soon as I got home from school, I went upstairs (Nannie was at the grocery store) and pushed the bassinet down the long hallway to my bedroom and positioned it right next to my bed. Thank goodness, we lived in a big house, as it wasn't until the next day when Mom and the baby were coming home, that she noticed the switch. By then, she had neither the time nor the inclination to discuss the sleeping arrangements of the new baby, with her headstrong granddaughter. With a shrug of her shoulders and pursed lips, she whispered, "My goodness, that little girl has a mind of her own."

Chapter Forty-one
Another Addition to Our Family—a puppy

It was about time that we finally got around to talking about getting a puppy. We were all settled into our new house and my parents were managing the insurance business without any major snafus. Dad had his cat Missy (Miss Boots) and, I should mention, we also had a new baby brother. It was high time that we talked dog. Conspicuously missing from this family was man's best friend. We needed a pup that was both furry and friendly and ferocious at times, the perfect companion for children, the front line of protection from strangers and dangers, a foot warmer on cold nights and a swimming buddy at the cottage. Indeed, we were missing a dog.

We brought Shep home in a cardboard box when he was just six weeks old. He was nothing more than a round fluffy ball of coal-black fur, ebony eyes, and a blackish nose. Everything was tiny about him but his paws. His paws were huge. My father nervously mentioned, "This is going to be a big dog when he grows up" and that was okay with Mom. She liked big dogs and she really liked German Shepherds. Shep was perfect.

Shep grew into his paws at a lightning pace. As soon as his food dish hit the floor, he was on it. He sucked every, last kibble out of the bowl like my mother's Hoover sucked up Cheerios that littered the kitchen floor around my sister's highchair. We used the "drop and run" technique when feeding him and he would not hesitate to growl out of the side of his mouth if someone was foolish enough to wander too close.

Within six months, Sheppie had grown by leaps and bounds and had most definitely become a force to be reckoned with. He had morphed from roly-poly puppy into a specimen that one might imagine of his breed. For the most part, he was a very good boy. He was gentle as could be with my baby brother and wonderfully loyal and attentive. Yes, he kept my feet warm as he curled up at the foot of my bed on cold winter nights and he loved our weekend trips to the cottage. His days were spent chasing an unsuspecting Canada goose, leaping off the dock for a quick swim in the lake and just being a dog.

There was, however, a problem with just being a dog. Dogs can become overly protective and territorial, staking out a claim to their house, their family, their porch, their yard. And if by some terrible lapse in judgement, some unsuspecting soul did stray too close to any of the above, there would be serious barking. Barking that was deep and resonating, barking that you knew came from a big dog. When a big dog barks, in this case a German shepherd, there are few options. You either quickly exit or risk something much worse than an angry curled lip and protruding canines.

Very early on, Shep exhibited some aggressive tendencies. To avoid any confrontation between dog and stranger, we were instructed to be particularly vigilant when we were going out the front door. The front door was Shep's gateway to mayhem. The front door led to the porch, the sidewalk and strangers. Strangers that in his doggie brain meant burglars, thieves and mass murderers. He had no choice but to protect his family. It was unfortunate, however, that the distinction between private property and public became a tad blurred as our front porch led directly to the sidewalk that was well traveled by you guessed it, strangers.

Sheppie had the perfect vantage point for watching the comings and goings of all the foot traffic that tromped down the hill in the morning and then back up the hill in the late afternoon. Glued to the dining room window, he took on the image of a stone still statue. Never moving, never barking, just his eyes rolling from side to side as he followed each, and every person, up the hill and down the hill.

There were groups of school kids with back packs and lunch boxes. There was an old couple that made a daily trip to town for provisions. There were two sisters that worked at the five and dime. And then there was John Cassidy.

John Cassidy was a handsome young lawyer who lived on the street above us. Every day he walked to his office on Decatur Street. I have no idea why, but Shep really, really did not like John Cassidy walking by our house. You could tell from his doggie body language that he prayed for an opportunity to confront his arch enemy, establish his Alpha dominance and settle things once and for all.

It was only a matter of time before Shep made his move. All he needed was a split second of carelessness, a door left ajar just long enough for his great escape. It was no surprise that he was always cruising the front hallway, ever vigilant, ever ready.

He exited like a blur of fur, pushing past my sister, air born from porch to sidewalk. His timing was impeccable. I wouldn't say that John Cassidy screamed. Men don't scream. But this was darn close. Mother rushed outside, part woman of the house, part alpha dog, part nurse. She commanded Shep to return to the porch and with apologies flying, approached our wounded neighbor. Thank goodness, the bite was superficial, but Mom insisted on taking him down to Doc Murphy's office just as a precaution. He graciously declined and hobbled the rest of the way up the hill.

That night at dinner, we got the "if Sheppie gets out again" talk as Dad warned us that if there were any more biting incidences, our dog could be deemed dangerous and be put to sleep. "Dangerous, Shep dangerous? What a ridiculous notion! There was nothing dangerous about our dog!" However much we protested, the reality was that Shep's aggressive tendencies were well documented and the next time might be the last straw.

Chapter Forty-two
A Box with a Picture—television comes to our house

If I came right home from school and finished my homework lickity split, Mom might let me go to a friend's house to play. I loved going to Lorie Knapp's house on Fifth Street. She had a super nice mom who let us run in the house, jump on the beds and play music real loud. Best of all, she made chocolate chip cookies almost every day and she didn't even make us wash our hands before we gobbled them up. There were definite advantages to not having a nurse for a mother.

Lorie's house was close by, only ten minutes away, down the hill to Franklin Street. Franklin Street was the hub of our village, our main street where rows of near century old buildings housed businesses that provided services and goods for the towns' people. Anchored to one of the four corners was the Jefferson Hotel and then, like conjoined twins, the barber, the bakery, the pharmacy, a ladies' dress shop, an ice cream parlor and Jimmie's Radio.

I had to walk right past Jimmie's Radio on my way to Lorie's house. On one such occasion, I noticed something quite unusual in the front window. It was a box that had dials on the front and meshy stuff on the side just like a radio but this was different. In the center of the box was a small rectangular glass screen and there was a young housewife holding a box of laundry detergent and words that flashed across the screen, "Nothing Gets Your Clothes Cleaner than Oxydol". Curiosity enticed me to push open the store's heavy oak door and I stuck my head in just far enough to take a quick peek at the talking picture in the box and just long enough for one of the Fazzio brothers to spot me and holler, "Tell your dad to get down here and buy a television for the family. Tell him to hurry...they're going fast! I got just ten in the first shipment and I've already sold four of them." This was unbelievable, a radio with a picture!

Later that night, I paced from window to window hoping to catch a glimpse of my father's headlights. Hoping that he would soon be home and I could tell him about the television. Hoping that he would be so excited that we would throw on our coats, leave dinner simmering on the stove and go straight away to Jimmy's Radio. I tried to share my exciting news with my mother, but she was much too busy mixing up a meat loaf while jiggling my baby brother on her hip.

Nannie had taught me that timing was everything when you wanted something from a man. Never ask for anything when the man of the house was tired or in a hurry or heaven forbid...hungry. I patiently watched as my dad chewed a bite of meatloaf, a forkful of mashed potatoes, munched on some carrot strips and finally dessert. I was dumbfounded that any human being could eat this slowly. When he had finished every, last drop of his chocolate pudding and I was positive that he was no longer hungry, it was time. He sat stoically, listening to my tale of the television, about what I saw at Jimmie's Radio and the salesman that had said that they were flying off the shelves. Certainly, we didn't want to be the only family in Watkins Glen without a television. That would indeed be too humiliating. By now, Dad had a big old grin on his face. "Hold on missy, hold on. Go up and look in the back of the station wagon." That's all he said.

That's all he had to say.

Chapter Forty-three

Television Shows for Everyone—entertainment in the 1950s

Mother was not about to allow that ugly box to take center stage in her lovely Victorian living room and had found the perfect spot for it in a much smaller room off the kitchen. This room was already the home of Dad's ugly brown tweed Barcalounger and other outcasts that Mother had brought from Lovell Avenue. As it turned out, this was indeed the perfect spot for the newly acquired television.

After hiking up the hill after school, I would come in the house, using the side door which led directly into the kitchen, where my mother would have a snack waiting for me on the counter. If I was careful not to make a mess, I could enjoy my peanut butter and jelly sandwich perched on a foot stool in front of the TV.

Inches from the screen, I waited for the announcer's voice to ask the question that every kid in America knew the answer to, "Boys and girls, what time is it?" And in response every kid in America shouted at their television screen, "IT'S HOWDY DOODY TIME!"

The cast was comprised of Howdy Doody, a wooden puppet with a shock of red hair and the bridge of his nose flecked with giant matching freckles, Buffalo Bob the ventriloquist, and Clarabelle the Clown. A group of raucous children, called the peanut gallery, sat on bleachers on the stage with Howdy Doody and his gang.

These had to be the luckiest kids in the whole world! I dreamed that, one day, I might be sitting on the bleachers singing "It's Howdy Doody Time, it's Howdy Doody Time", set to the tune of Ta-rah-rah Boom-de-ay. Dream on little girl, dream on.

The show had a western theme with Howdy Doody and Buffalo Bob in plaid shirts and cowboy kerchiefs. There was Clarabelle the Clown, who never spoke but communicated by squeezing the rubber ball of a bicycle horn. This worked quite well with simple yes or no answers but was a bit more challenging for any conversation beyond that. It all seemed to work. I mean seriously, what's not to love, a puppet and his pal dressed in western regalia.

After dinner there was a mad scramble to the newly designated "TV room" as the children jockeyed for position on the blue tweed sectional. There was most definitely, a hierarchy in place. No one sat in Dad's Barcalounger. That was a sacred place, a modern throne of its time, reserved for the patriarch of the family, the boss, the breadwinner, the head of the household.

Mom had her favorite spot, curled up on the end of the couch with one of her new TV tables, within arm's reach, juxtaposed between the couch and the kitchen in case she had to make a mad dash to grab an ice tea for Dad.

Just as there was nothing democratic about our seating arrangement, there was also nothing democratic about what shows we were going to watch. My father enjoyed "Gun Smoke", "Wagon Train", "Bonanza", manly man shows about the Wild West and gun slinging sheriffs who were hell-bent on law and order. Shows with blazing bullets and billowing clouds of dust from galloping horses. Fortunately, I had cowboy in my "blood", so I was totally on board with this playbill.

Variety shows were also a big hit with my parents. Probably one of the most popular was the Ed Sullivan Show. Every Sunday night he would saunter onto the stage from behind an impressive velvet curtain. An odd little man in a rumpled suit, with his arms crisscrossed over his chest like an Indian chief at a pow-wow and with a slurry mumble announce with all certainty that tonight would be a really, big "shoooo".

An appearance on the Ed Sullivan Show would almost guarantee stardom for young up-and-coming musicians, singers and comedians.

On one such Sunday night in 1956, when I was in the throes of pubescence, a handsome young southern boy, in a way-too-flashy sports jacket and slicked back hair, was introduced to his soon-to-be throngs of screaming, trembling, tears-rolling-down-their-cheeks admirers.

His name was Elvis...Elvis Presley. His style was like no other. His voice was deep and lilted with shades of gospel and a whole lot of rock and roll. His popularity was not just about his pipes or his musical prowess. You didn't just listen to Elvis. You listened and you watched. You watched his gyrations, the sensual rolling of his hips in perfect rhythm, arms flailing across the strings of his guitar. The visual was way too much for the time. Too sexy...way too sexy. The

1950's in America was all about modesty, privacy, piety, and keeping all things sexual in a tight little tucked away place.

It was not surprising that prime time broadcasters were not ready for this phenomenon. Consequently, Elvis' first appearance only revealed him from the waist up for the television audience. Imagine the curiosity of all who were watching when we not only heard Elvis belt out "Love Me Tender" and watched him shake his upper torso, but heard the screams of the live audience who were privy to the waist down action as well.

The 1950's would never be the same. I would never be the same. Music in America would never be the same.

Chapter Forty-four
School is Out- a new routine

The summers were long and hot and uneventful in many a small town in upstate New York and where I lived was no exception. We still made occasional trips to the cottage, but Mom and Dad were very busy with the insurance business and their growing involvement in the community. Most days, I spent time on the front porch reading books and playing with the cat. Nannie would come for the day and she would make banana and peanut butter sandwiches and a big jug of bug juice. I'm not really sure what constitutes the term "bug juice" but it's part Kool aid, part orange juice (or whatever juice was in the fridge) some lemon slices (or whatever fruit was in the fridge) lots of ice and a warm summer breeze to meld this sugary libation to perfection.

I would spread an old blanket in the tall grass in the backyard and sit cross-legged, munching and slurping and licking the mashed banana and peanut butter concoction from between my fingers. It wouldn't be long before I was joined by an army of ants marching doggedly through the folds in search of a crumb.

Also joining the picnic were giant, pea green grasshoppers. There were bumble bees with their yellow and black fuzzy coats and pollen laden legs. There were dragon flies, their wings all translucent with colors of a rainbow. And lastly, there were angle worms that eagerly poked their heads out of a mound of moist earth. No, this was not a solitary place and I most certainly was not alone.

The setting sun signaled the end to the scorching heat and an invitation to all the neighborhood to scurry into the street for a game of "kick the can" or "freeze tag" or "hide and seek". I would gobble my dinner and ever so politely ask to be excused, trying hard not to appear too anxious before making my great escape.

There was precious little time before the streetlights flickered a signal that it was time to come in the house. I learned, in years prior, that it would be foolhardy to ignore said signal and try to explain that you had somehow not noticed the sudden illumination of the entire block. Foolhardy because the next night you would be watching the games from the lonely vantage point of your bedroom window. A lesson learned.

The highlight of the summer street games had nothing to do with tag or hide and seek but rather about chasing after the village truck that was spraying for mosquitos. I'd spot it first, as it lumbered down the street coughing up gray white clouds of bug killing pesticide. You had to be a fast runner and the ability to hold your breath for a very long time or you'd be swallowed up by the toxic fog bank. Lucky for me, I had racehorse legs and the lungs of a baleen whale. I could run and hold my breath with the best of them.

I'm sure that Mother would have been horrified if she had ever suspected that her firstborn was engaged in such a foolish exercise in stupidity. Thank heavens, she never did.

I dodged the bullet on that one.

Chapter Forty-five
Summer was About to Change—finding a new friend

One of the best things about summer vacation was not having to get up, get dressed, gobble down a bowl of cereal, and for most of the year, bundle up and be out the door by 7:30 AM.

School was finished for another year and I was free, liberated from the trials and tribulations that were associated with all things concerning my education.

Instead, most mornings, I was content to linger a bit longer in bed, swaddled in my favorite softy blanket. I was a butterfly wrapped in a wooly chrysalis...all warm and toasty. Mom agreed to let me sleep all night with the window open even though she had concerns about street noise waking me and my getting a chill. I must admit, that by morning, with my venetian blinds pulled up and the curtains flapping like a crazy parrot, it was a bit nippy.

I probably would have stayed put a while longer, but the tantalizing smell of bacon frying and English muffins in the toaster, was not to be ignored. I was the proverbial blood hound, nose to the ground, as I sniffed my way down the stairs, through a labyrinth of rooms, until I was standing next to the stove. I found myself staring into the cast iron fry pan that was spitting and spattering bacon grease like an angry medieval dragon. Mother had donned her apron and with weapon (a metal spatula) in hand was ready for battle. The dragon (bacon) was slain and soon lay all crispy on my plate.

Mom soon joined me at the oversized round oak table that dominated one corner of the kitchen. "Did you notice that there is a strange car parked on the street in front of the old Chapman house? Go have a look. It's a brand-new Cadillac, baby blue and white, with Eldorado embossed on the side. And it has a Florida license plate. Go have a look!"

I had to admit that I was a bit curious, but I didn't want to look like a busybody, a snoopy ole neighbor. What could I possibly be doing in my pajamas, standing in the middle of Monroe Street at eight o'clock in the morning that would not be perceived as just a tad weird?

After some back and forth with my mother, I found myself standing in the middle of the empty street. I was preparing to turn on my heels and make a mad dash for the side door, when a girl, that seemed to be right around my age, peeked out from behind an enormous baby blue tail fin. She looked equally embarrassed and confessed, "My grandmother made me come down to the car to fetch her reading glasses from the glove compartment. My name is Lynn. Lynn Duncan. I just arrived last night, and I will be spending the summer here."

There was no doubt that we were going to become close friends as we stood in the middle of the street at eight o'clock in the morning and we both were wearing our pajamas.

I scurried back to the house with precious details of my reconnaissance mission. Someone my age...someone to play with...no more boring summer days. I had to act quickly, strike while the iron was hot, before she became best friends with someone else.

I rummaged through my dresser drawer tossing the rejected shirts and shorts in a pile. I was looking for the perfect outfit. Something without grass stains and not too flashy. Something new that didn't look new. Something without rips or tears or dog slobber. Heaven forbid, I didn't want to appear desperate.

The plan was that I would go over to her house and after some chit chat, I would suggest, ever so casually, that maybe she could come over and play some Chinese checkers on my front porch.

It was exactly twelve steps from the end of our sidewalk to the street and then an additional twenty steps from there to Lynn's front door. I started out at a pretty good clip but by the time I reached the street and gazed up at the towering old red brick mansion, I became very, very nervous. I imagined that the giant oak trees in front of her house, were waving their branches at me and their twisted bark mouths were screaming, "Stay away little girl! Go home little girl!" I struggled to climb the stairs to her front porch. It seemed like there were huge globs of bubble gum stuck to the soles of my shoes. Every step took superhuman effort as if I had forgotten how to walk.

At last, I reached the massive front doors. Intimidating to say the least. Panes of hundred-year-old stained and beveled glass filled the porch with a rainbow of color. I searched for the doorbell and gave it a quick tap. There was so much noise in my head that I really didn't know if it had alerted the occupants inside. I waited and waited, but no luck. No one came to the door. I made a fist and gently rapped and that's when the door opened with a jerk.

A diminutive, somewhat chubby, old woman, with a tight little bun on the top of her head and wearing a housecoat covered with a well-worn, flowered cotton apron, was all that stood between me and a new-found friendship. The perfect antidote to a boring summer. Her expression was tolerant, bordering on impatient, when she queried "What do you want young lady?"

I'd come this far, too far to turn back now.

Lynnie and I spent the summer together with long afternoons lounging on the front porch, drinking bug juice and eating peanut butter and jelly sandwiches.

Mom ran an extension cord out of the living room window so there was power for my record player. Barefooted, we whirled and twirled and strummed and gyrated to the spinning vinyl discs. One stacked on top of the other waiting for their turn. There was Elvis. There were the Everly Brothers. There was Fats Domino. They were right there with Lynnie and me on my front stoop, on any given warm summer day, circa 1958.

It's true that, most days, I would be the first to take my position in front of the Parcheesi board waiting for my friend to roll out of bed, but on one particular morning things were quite the opposite.

I was still all snuggy when I heard Lynn calling me from the street outside my bedroom window. "You have to get out here right away! It's unbelievable! It's too good to be true! You'll never guess!" Well, she was right about that. I had absolutely no idea what she was talking about. I threw on a pair of shorts and yesterday's tank top and scurried outside. By the time I reached the street, my friend had lost all sense of self composure. She was leaping and yelping and waving her arms like a loonie. "Calm down", I pleaded. "I can't understand a thing that you're saying. Calm down." After considerable deliberation I was able to figure out just two words that she was saying, Elvis and movie. That's about all that I could decipher between the squeals and screams and tears. Seriously? Now, I thought that Elvis was cute, and his gyrations were way sexy, and his voice was unique, and his songs put the rock in rock and roll, but this was ridiculous.

That night we got all gussied up. Poodle skirts, crinolines, white bucks, ponytails. Lynn had smuggled a tube of Ruby Passion lipstick from her mom's makeup case that we smeared on our lips as soon as we were away from our houses.

It's not surprising that we were the first in line at the Glen Theatre downtown. Actually there was no line at all. "What's the matter with this town? Don't they realize that this is the premier of "King Creole" starring the one and only Elvis Presley?" I tried to reassure her that everything was going to be OK. That this was a small town with a rather conservative population, and I was sure that more people would be arriving soon. We blasted by the popcorn and milk duds, down the center aisle and plopped, center stage, in the front row. Lynn was unusually subdued, and I actually complimented her on her composure, her self- restraint. Unfortunately for me, that was all about to change.

The theatre went dark, the much larger than life MGM lion roared, and the words King Creole splashed across the silver screen. There he was, singing and shaking and strumming with his hair all flopping back and forth. It was too much. It was way too much for my friend. She leapt out of her seat and started screaming at the top of her lungs.

For the next hour and twenty-two minutes she did not stop screaming. I was speechless. I was mortified. I wanted to go home, say goodbye to my parents and move to Iceland. But Lynnie was my friend and I always knew that she was different. Different from my school friends or the other kids that lived on my street. I just had to be brave, suck it up and as soon as the light came up at the movie's end, hightail it out of there before anyone recognized me. Fat chance that would happen.

September came way too soon. On the dreaded day, I crouched on the floor, barely peeking over the sill of my bedroom window, as Lynn's father slung an oversized valise into the cavernous trunk of the Caddie. He scurried back to the house and returned with two more pieces of well-worn Samsonite, an assortment of hat boxes and shopping bags, a garment bag bulging with Mr. Duncan's gabardine suits and Mrs. Duncan's wool tweed blazers, a silky pink comforter from Lynnie's bed, cardboard boxes of records and books.

This was the day that my summer friend, my constant companion for more than three months, was leaving me. We had said our goodbyes the day before, promising to write every single day. There was desperate talk about becoming blood sisters before she left. Lynn had found an old hat pin of her grandmothers and we dipped the point into a bottle of alcohol (my idea) before we quickly poked our index fingers. Two tiny streams of blood smooshed together would seal the deal.

We would be friends for life.

Chapter Forty-six
Tante Marries at Last—Nannie tells me why

Tante had married and moved to Skokie, Illinois a sprawling bedroom community of Chicago, where she secured a teaching position in the city. My Uncle Joe, her new husband, was a Kentucky native, and a retired Lieutenant Colonel in the Air Force. He was smart (he had a PHD in Engineering) and designed and built ten-unit apartment buildings in the bedroom communities that surrounded the bustling metropolis. He was much older than she and yet, not a bad looking fellow. Reserved and soft spoken with his southern drawl and quite pleasant. Nannie said that he was old enough to be her father (he was never forthcoming with his age) but my aunt seemed quite happy and paid no attention to my grandmother's grousing.

One day, I asked Nannie why Tante had married so much later than my mother and she shared this story with me.

Yolanda Hewitt (Tante) was twenty years old and attending Elmira College, a prestigious women's university where she had an impeccable GPA and tutored those who were less capable in Latin and French. She also worked in the campus library to earn extra money to offset the cost of tuition and books. Thankfully, the campus was just a short bus ride from Herrick Street (she could even walk if she was so inclined) which made it possible for her to live at home and save the expense of living on campus.

It was at the library that she met the young man who would ultimately be the first love of her life. His name was Gregory

Birmingham, a tall lanky fellow with piercing green eyes, a pasty white complexion and a shock of jet-black, ramrod straight hair, desperately in need of a barber's scissors. And ears that were way too big for his head. His well-worn London Fog trench coat hinted of old money but the rest of his ensemble was a rumpled mess.

Tante was sitting at the huge mahogany information desk that stood guard at the library's entrance. It was one of her duties to watch the comings and goings of the students and to direct them to wherever they needed to go. It would be less than forthcoming to say that my aunt didn't notice the young man pass by.

 At first, he walked with a sense of purpose but all too soon, it was obvious that he was in need of some assistance. Yolanda stood up, abandoning her post, and with her most bookish self-reliant demeanor walked across the marble floor to where he was standing. His hands were pushed down in his pants pockets and those same beautiful eyes were roaming across the coffered ceiling. "Can I help you find something?", "Are you looking for something in particular?", "Have you ever been here before?"

That was the beginning of what would become a friendship and eventually a romance. A romance that was not without obstacles. You see Gregory Birmingham was Roman Catholic. Yes, he was Irish and you would have thought that would have been a good thing considering the fact that Nannie and Pa were just one generation from the Emerald Isle. But we were Protestant Irish, Orange Irish and the

Birminghams were Catholic, Green Irish with the Pope and centuries of bad blood between the warring factions.

In spite of the efforts of both of the families to discourage the young lovers, their romance flourished. All the meddling and scheming to keep them apart seemed only to strengthen their resolve. They talked about getting married. They talked about having children, traveling to exotic far-away places, buying a pretty little clapboard house with a white picket fence or maybe a farmhouse with a barn and chickens. And a tractor and a vegetable garden. And dogs and cats that would tromp through the garden and sleep in the barn. They were young and there seemed to be nothing that could possibly diminish their passion, their commitment to each other, their love for each other.

The Birminghams lived in Wellsboro, Pennsylvania just an hour or so from Elmira. The family owned a well-established and profitable manufacturing company that was waiting for Gregory to finish school and join the father and two uncles at the helm of the operation. The elders were all getting well on in years and it wouldn't be long before the gauntlet would be passed and the business would belong to Greg.

The plan for a spring wedding was announced one wintery February evening, as the family partook in a traditional pot roast and gravy supper. Gregory had been invited to stay for dinner and it seemed like a perfect opportunity to break the news. Tante had let her younger sister in on the scheme as they prepared a united front. Young love versus generations of religious intolerance.

Gregory began with the traditional pledge of love and devotion for his prospective bride. Tante assured her worried parents that their fears were for naught. They would marry and have children and a fabulous life and they would somehow figure out the whole religion debacle when faced with it in the future.

By the time the discussion had run its course, the mashed potatoes looked like wallpaper paste and the gravy had congealed on the plates. In the end, they gave their blessing, even though their own parents, who came to this country for religious freedom, were most likely rolling over in their graves. Certainly, Gregory would be able to financially take care of their first-born daughter. He was a young man of good character and moral integrity, from a family that was highly respected. In almost every way, he would make a fine husband.

While all of this was going on inside, Mother Nature was busy outside. A generous dusting of gigantic snowflakes had turned everything into a monochromatic winter wonderland. With the wind picking up, it made all this whiteness swirl into icy dust devils that made visibility near zero.

Quickly, Gregory threw on his coat and after a perfunctory peck on the cheek of each of the women present, headed toward his car parked at the curb. Tante stood in the doorway breathing warmly on the frosty storm door and watched the old Studebaker sputter down Herrick Street and disappear into the mix of dark and snowiness.

It was five-thirty the next morning, when the house was awakened by the ringing of the phone. There was an immediate sense of panic as Nannie rushed downstairs, hoping that her fears would soon be put to rest. She hoped that it was someone who had sleepily dialed the wrong number, or a telephone prank being made by some silly child who had snuck out of bed before his parents were awake.

The robotic voice of a Pennsylvania State Police dispatcher gave the grim details of what had happened. The storm had made the mountainous road to Wellsboro particularly treacherous the night before. A couple was driving south when the snow really started to come down. So much so that they decided to pull over to the side of the road until it let up a bit. It was from this vantage point that they saw headlights barely visible from the bottom of a ravine. The concerned driver left the car and after crawling through some heavy brush trudged down the side of the hill. Even in the darkness, he knew what he was looking at. The car was upside down, its tires sticking straight up. There was a stream of hot, soon to be cold steam spewing out from under the hood. Headlights, half buried in the snow, gave the whole scene an eerie illusion of something gone very, very wrong. As he came closer to the car, he could see that it was a gray car. A gray Studebaker and Gregory Birmingham was dead inside.

Chapter Forty-seven
Flying solo—a trip to Chicago to visit Tante and Uncle Joe

Tante and Uncle Joe had been living in a suburb of Chicago for several years and were well established in their new digs. They had mentioned to mother that they would love for me to come for a visit during my summer vacation. The plan was that I would fly from Buffalo airport aboard a turbo prop Capital Viscount, spend two weeks with my aunt and uncle and return home on a flight from Chicago to Buffalo.

"Of course, I was old enough to fly by myself! What was the big deal?" Mom and Dad would put me on the plane and Tante and Uncle Joe would be waiting at the gate at O'Hare. There were stewardesses, looking all stylish in their uniforms, who were more than capable of looking after a teenager for two hours. After all, I wasn't going anywhere. I was most certainly not going to get lost between row 1 A and row 14 B. To my knowledge, a kid had never been misplaced at fifteen thousand feet. I would be fine, just fine.

One thing was for certain. I could not go to the Windy City with the same old, same old that I had hanging in my closet. Nannie and I had to make a special trip over town to purchase the perfect outfits for travel and sightseeing. This would not be cheap. No Iszard's or Sheehan's for this fashion mission. There would be no discounts or mark downs or stuff that was on sale. We were going for the good stuff.

We went straight to Gorton Coy where dresses screamed pricey. This was a trip of a lifetime and I was counting on the fact that I would be hundreds of miles away when mother got the bill. I was also quite sure that Nannie would be able to make perfect sense of our extravagant shopping trip.

Our search was a fruitful one, a total success. Nannie and I returned with bags overflowing. Bags full of party dresses and sun dresses and soft cardigans and skirts in the latest hues and cotton blouses that would complete each ensemble.

I woke up early on the day of my flight, staggered into the bathroom, where I smeared a glob of green speckled toothpaste onto a well chewed toothbrush and scrubbed away. "Brusha, brusha, brusha, new Ipana toothpaste!" the jingle from the television commercial swam in my head. Next it was the meticulous chore of removing the mess of prickly rollers that covered my head. Three across the top, two on each side and four in the back. It was not easy being beautiful and I had to pray for zero humidity or by noon I would look like Medusa the snake woman.

The sundress that I would be traveling in was Nannie's favorite. It was a shiny cotton fabric, slightly off-white with some tiny little navy blue Fleur de Lis designs all over the full skirt. The bodice was empire with a silky gray ribbon that tied under where my breasts would be some day.

Then there were navy flats, a lightweight cardigan in case it was chilly on the plane, my emerald birthstone ring and a charm bracelet laden with charms. A ballerina, a pair of toe shoes, a basketball, a golf club (from Dad), a cheerleader's megaphone, a heart, roller skates, ice skates, a birthday cake, a Christmas tree, a dog (Sheppie), a cat (Missy) and on and on and on.

I had hidden a tube of pinkish, orange coral lipstick in my pocket for future application and Mother had insisted that I put on a pretty little pair of white gloves (her words, not mine) because that's what well-bred, young ladies wore when they traveled. So said Emily Post, the guru of good manners, the proper etiquette expert, and Mom's role model, mentor and downright hero. No one can argue with that resume.

The whole family packed into Dad's station wagon for the trip to the airport. Dad was behind the wheel and Mother was right next to him in the front seat. Nannie and Pa were bookends with me in the middle and my sister and brother had crawled into the cargo space in the rear where Dad had put my suitcase.

The trip itself was uneventful and we arrived at the airport with time to spare. It had been decided that Mom and Dad would take me to the gate where airline officials had told them that they would be allowed to escort me onto the plane. The gate was in the center of the terminal and as we hurried down the main corridor to our destination, we noticed a large crowd of people all milling around precisely where we were going. As we got closer and were able to get a better look, it was apparent that I was going to have a wonderful flight to Chicago and most assuredly to my parent's chagrin, they knew I was right. This particular flight was used by the military to carry new recruits to the training base in the Great Lakes.

Yes indeed, a plane full of young sailors and me.

Chapter Forty-eight

Adventures in the Windy City—what fun I had with Tante

There they were, standing on the edge of a roped off area, just a few feet from the tarmac. As all the passengers filed off of the plane, I was conspicuous by my appearance and stood out like a coquettish young girl in a sea of starched white uniforms. Tante and Uncle Joe spotted me right away.

After grabbing my suitcase from the carousel, we headed straight to the short-term parking. Tante and I huddled in the backseat of Uncle Joe's Lincoln Continental talking girl talk and school talk and chattering about where we were going to go and what we were going to see and eat and buy and experience and explore. There would be Marshall Fields for shopping and restaurants in Old Town. There were museums, it seemed, on almost every corner and parks with the most beautiful Romanesque fountains with marble stallions romping in a perpetual mist. Quite the contrast from the tiny hamlet in upstate New York that I had left just a few hours before.

Before we got to the apartment, we made a stop at the local supermarket to pick up some groceries. I had often gone shopping with Mother, but I had never experienced anything like this. The frozen food aisle stretched the entire length of the store. It was miles long and towering freezers, jammed packed with all things frozen, lined both sides of the aisle. For some reason, they reminded me of ice-covered glass skyscrapers similar to what I had seen in a New York City travel brochure.

My aunt had given me carte blanche, the proverbial blank check, permission to pick out three ice cream treats. Not one. Not two. Three ice cream treats that were all mine. I didn't have to share them with my sister or brother or my father. Nope, they were just for me. Could a vacation have had any better of a start?

I woke bright and early the next morning, wrapped myself in my softy robe and headed to the kitchen. Tante, dressed in a pretty little cotton housecoat, was busily flipping pancakes on a cast iron griddle that I was quite certain came from Herrick Street.

Uncle Joe was Mr. Suit and Tie, ready for a day at the office. He looked dapper in a brown tweed jacket with leather patches on the elbows, a fresh from the laundry, white shirt and a chocolate colored bow tie. My dad always wore a tie when he went to the office, but I had never seen a real live person wear a bow tie. Once, I saw Fred Astaire wear one in a movie and he really looked cool and so did my Uncle Joe.

After breakfast it was time to tidy up. I volunteered to wash the dishes, something that I never did at home. Why is it so much less of a chore to wash dishes at someone else's house? Hopefully there would be no mention of my good deed or how helpful I was being when Tante spoke to Mother on the telephone. It was a quick shower and off to catch the train.

The L, short for elevated, would take us to the city and there was a station just a few blocks from the apartment. We had waited until midmorning to avoid the throngs of worker bees swarming into Chicago's financial district and beyond. My aunt was very familiar with the train's schedule as she rode back and forth on it Monday through Friday when school was in session.

We had barely time to purchase our tickets and position ourselves on the edge of the platform when a train came roaring toward us. Suddenly, it threw on its brakes, as if it recognized an old friend and came to a screeching, squealing stop, right in front of us.

Once on board, we had little time to find a seat before the train lurched forward, anxious to get on to the next station. I was reminded of Louis Carroll's White Rabbit. "I'm late, I'm late for a very important date." We sped along the track with a gentle rocking to and fro, a click and a clack, having the perfect vantage point of the city.

The buildings were a delightful blur of grays and blacks and steel and concrete and brick. As the train slowed, I could see that there were shops and restaurants and gas stations, and an occasional green space thrown into the mix. The sidewalks were overflowing with people busily going somewhere and yellow taxis and city buses, covered with giant advertisements, all jockeying for position. There were probably more people in that one square block than the entire population of Watkins Glen, New York.

Tante grabbed my hand as the train approached Michigan Avenue and we were pushed along with the crowd, until we were finally able to break loose on the sidewalk outside of the station.

I scurried along as fast as my toothpick legs could carry me, with a firm grip on my aunt's hand. When I finally had the presence of mind to look up, we were standing in front of a bank of massive brass trimmed doors. The plate glass, so dazzling that one might have thought that there was no glass there at all, except for the swirled initials M F elegantly embossed on the center pane.

I was about to enter paradise, a department store, the likes that I had never seen. I was about to enter the portals of Marshal Fields. There seemed to be only one apparent way in. That was through the revolving doors that swirled at break-neck speeds, with eager shoppers entering and contented shoppers exiting. It was apparent, that timing was of the essence. Was I brave enough to venture in sans aunt, or would I cling to her like a sticky burr on a mangy dog's belly? I chose the latter.

A rush of perfumed air swept up my nostrils, as we escaped the confines of the revolving door and I found myself, front and center, in the cosmetics department. A white marble floor, so shiny, it looked like it was still wet from mopping, welcomed us to come hither. There were counters, after counters, after counters of perfumes galore and lipsticks of every shade and powders to keep the shine off your nose. There was Chanel No 5, Estee Lauder, Tabu, Joy, and my mother's favorite, Shalimar by Guerlain. As I made my way down the aisle, I dabbed, I sprayed, I sniffed, I even splattered. When there was not a centimeter of unscented flesh on either of my forearms, I acquiesced to my aunt's request to move on to the teen department in search of something dressy that I could wear to the Kungsholm for our special night out on Friday.

The Kungsholm was both a restaurant and a theatre, housed in what was once a magnificent mansion at the corner of Rush and Ontario streets, just off Chicago's Miracle Mile. In its previous life it had been the private residence of the wealthy McCormick family, but it had been reconfigured to create two separate spaces for the Kungsholm.

On the left, there was the dining room that was dominated by a mile-long banquet table. A heavily starched linen cloth puddled on the floor and silver trays and cut glass bowls held the contents of an elegant, sumptuous, authentic Swedish smorgasbord.

I followed my aunt's lead as she carried a tiny plate around the perimeter of the table. You always start with the cold items. It was a dollop of pickled herring, sliced cucumbers dressed in vinegar, eel and cream cheese rolled into pinwheels, beet salad, boiled potatoes and smoked salmon.

Then it was a clean plate for the hot stuff, Swedish meatballs that you dipped in lingonberry jam and slabs of ham and turkey. Tante reminded me to save room for the sweet stuff. I

n the corner of the dining room there was a table of desserts. Pies and cakes and cookies and chocolates. Yes, you had to have a clean plate. I reminded myself that I would never volunteer to wash dishes at this place.

When everyone could hold not another morsel, we filed across the hall into the theatre section which was even more elegant. It was classic, turn of the century, opulence with brocade wallpaper and gilded filigree on the spiral staircase and around all the doorways. Thick carpets on the floor and midnight blue velvet curtains were draped across the ceiling to floor windows.

Once inside the theatre, there was more velvet drawn across the stage, more velvet on the rows of chairs and more golden filigree everywhere. The light from crystal-laden chandeliers washed over the entire room and gave everything it touched a palatial quality.

Tante had explained to me that I was about to experience something quite unique. The Kungsholm was not only famous for its Swedish smorgasbord, but also for its productions of puppet operas. It seemed like a rather odd, but intriguing concept. I think that once I had listened to Caruso singing Carmen on a recording, but this was different. For a teenage girl, who listened to Elvis and Buddy Holly, opera was just a bunch of warbling and not even warbling in English but Italian warbling. I was about to be pleasantly surprised.

There were giant stringed marionettes, all decked out in lovely costumes, looking much like their human counterparts at the Met in New York City or La Scala in Milan. The first thing that I noticed was the orchestra pit, filled with black gowned and tuxedo clad puppet musicians, all busily fine tuning their instruments in preparation for the evening's performance. The maestro bounced to the podium, bowed politely to the audience, raised his baton and without hesitation, beautiful music floated from the pit and drifted down the aisle toward us. The curtain slowly opened, and the magic began. For the next two hours, I sat mouth agape, not moving a muscle, not uttering a sound, somehow realizing that I would remember this for the rest of my life.

Chapter Forty-nine
Back to Reality—fishing on the St Lawrence River

In what seemed like the blink of an eye, I was walking down the tarmac to board the plane back to Buffalo, New York. I had almost reached the metal stairs, when I turned and waved to my aunt and uncle. They were standing in almost the exact spot, where I had first seen them two weeks ago. What a wonderful time, what an incredible experience. This was, indeed, a trip of a lifetime.

The entire clan was waiting for me when the mighty Viscount touched down with a screech of rubber against concrete, taxied down the runway and lumbered toward its destination directly in front of the entrance to gate five. My parents were relieved that, as I left the plane, there was not a single sailor to be seen. Just a middle-aged couple, a family with their brood, a young mother cradling her baby, businessmen with briefcases, a few tourists, the usual conglomeration.

We still had several weeks of summer vacation left and Mom and Dad were aching for a getaway. A fishing trip to their favorite fish camp on the St Lawrence River was just what the doctor ordered.

The following Saturday, everyone had to pitch in as we prepared for our trip. Mother was already in the kitchen, by sunrise, making an enormous pot of chili and a double batch of baking powder biscuits. Dad was in the basement collecting all the fishing poles and making sure that each had enough line, a proper hook and sinker. And we needed bait.

The night before, we had collected angleworms from the backyard by first putting on the sprinklers to draw the slimy creatures to the surface. After dark, with flashlight in hand, we scooped them up and tossed them into soil filled Planter's peanut cans.

There was always a competition to see who could capture the most worms. I would always try to grab the real fat and juicy ones, claiming that I was, most assuredly, the winner because my worms were twice as big as my sister's and father's. I suggested that we should judge, not by number captured, but by weight. To my chagrin, Dad would simply ignore the logic of my premise by patting me on the head and saying, "Nice try!" We would also need a bucket full of minnows, but we would wait until we got to Cape Vincent and buy some from the local bait store.

Suitcases and duffle bags and extra blankets and swim towels and the Coleman stove were all jammed into the back of the station wagon. Dad had a topper that held the fishing gear, camping paraphernalia, cooking utensils, boxes with kitchen staples (flour, salt, pepper, Crisco shortening) and a giant blue and white striped cooler filled with all the perishables. We did not travel light and it was not out of character that as my father trudged up the stairs to the car, for the umpteenth time, that he might have mentioned that Mother had packed everything but the kitchen sink. To which my mother's retort was always, "Don't tempt me!"

So, like little sausages, we were squeezed into our assigned spaces. I had my favorite softy pillow, my sister had her stuffed poodle, Fifi, and my baby brother was quite content perched on Mother's lap with a bottle full of apple juice.

The drive was uneventful and in just a couple of hours we were pulling up in front of Jesse Brink's fish camp on the St Lawrence River. There were no Michelin stars awarded to these accommodations. The cabins were old and somewhat rundown and void of any amenities. There was an outhouse nearby, running water in the kitchen sink, cots with paper thin mattresses and a picnic table out front.

But what was undeniably beautiful, was the view. Everywhere you looked there was water. Water splashing up against the dock, water rolling onto the shore, water that was a shade of blue black with white caps, water that looked deep and cold and foreboding and magical. There were pines and oaks and an abundance of rock. Tiny rocks that made a beach and huge boulders that held all the water at bay.

My parents were pros when it came to setting up camp. Our Spartan quarters were somehow morphed into a space that was quite comfortable. Tufted patchwork quilts and an assortment of sleeping bags and feather pillows were tossed on the cots. The pot of chili, bubbling on the camp stove, was spitting bits of tomato lava and the hotter it became, the more it roiled and boiled and took on the persona of some out of control volcano.

Dad was pretending to be busy setting up all the fishing equipment, but the truth be told, he had sought out Jesse, the camp owner, and they were talking fish talk. What was biting? What was the bait du jour? Who had caught the biggest bass, trout, pike? How many inches? How many pounds? The usual guy on a fishing trip talk.

We crawled into bed right after dinner and were put on notice that we would be rising with the sun. At dawn, I pulled on my oldest pair of jeans and my favorite red flannel shirt. After gobbling down a bowl of Rice Krispies, I ran to the water's edge and catapulted into Dad's trusty aluminum boat. I positioned myself between the bait bucket and the gas can so that there would be no room for my baby brother to sit next to me.

This was a very strategic and calculated move because he had the reputation of not being very seaworthy. The scenario was thus….cute little guy in a giant orange life jacket bouncing up and down and back and forth for hours on end. It was only a matter of time until his tiny tummy could take no more and whatever was left of his oatmeal and apple sauce was destined to be shared with anyone unlucky enough to be in close proximity.

When everyone had taken their position, we were off. The weather was cooperating, warm and not too windy. The river was calm with just a bit of a roll. The sky covered us like a great blue tablecloth with just a puff or two of cotton clouds. The motor sputtered along and soon we could no longer see the point of the fish camp. There was water and sky. There was greeny blue and wet and cold and deep beneath us and there was azure blue and sparkling warm above us. Both seemed to flow on forever.

In my father's world, fishing was serious business. Though we were told that this was going to be fun, we all knew better.

First off, there were rules. Just like the fishing rules that we had at the cottage, but there were even more rules here on the river.

Rule number one...there was no talking. Talking was forbidden. Something about fish having really good hearing. This seemed particularly odd to me considering the fact that I was quite sure that fish didn't even have ears. But that was a rule.

Rule number two...you had to keep your pole tip down. It was perilous to all aboard, if for some reason, you yanked your pole out of the water and it smacked someone in the face. Not good.

Which brings us to rule number three...once you had baited your hook and cast your line over the side of the boat, you then had to sit ramrod still with your thumb and forefinger tenderly holding the line and both of your eyes riveted to the red and white plastic bobber. You could only reel in your line if your bobber disappeared into the pitch-black water indicating that a fish had fallen for the old worm around the hook charade. It was time to reel in your catch. While you were reeling, you had to stay completely composed. No jerky movement. No yanking the pole in the air. No letting slack in your line. These rules were ridiculous.

How could you possibly remain cool, calm and collected when Moby Dick had just eaten your minnow!

But possibly the most challenging rule of all was rule number four. There would be no going back to the camp to go to the bathroom. There were no exceptions to this rule. You could wiggle, you could rock back and forth, you might grit your teeth or even squeeze out a tear but to no avail. We came to fish and nothing else...not even peeing. What was remarkable was the fact that the entire family had developed incredible, superhuman bladder control. Out of necessity, I presume.

It would not be unusual for us to be in the boat, pole tips down, in total silence without moving a muscle for six or seven hours at a time. Motoring to a favorite spot, throwing out the anchor, getting our poles in the water and then the wait. We rocked and we waited, and we waited and rocked. Up and down and down and up until I couldn't take it anymore.

When I determined that my father was not paying attention, preoccupied with a fish that had swallowed the hook or a line that was tangled in some seaweed, I would slowly start reeling in my line until my water logged worm, was all but begging for this torture to end, dangled inches from the water's surface. With feigned shocked amazement, I lamented that somehow my silly worm swam to the surface. I had no choice but to break rule number three and pull in my line and put on some new bait. This one was caput. It had wiggled its last wiggle and by all accounts had absolutely no appeal to any fish in the river.

Dad nodded in reluctant agreement, handed me my Planter's peanut can and mumbled something under his breath that sounded like "That kid has a mind of her own."

It turned out that this fishing expedition was of epic proportion. Luckily, we floated into a large school of beautiful yellow and mossy green striped perch. There were so many fish that you could potentially pull them by the handful from the icy water. We barely had time to throw a fresh worm or minnow on our hook before we were reeling another into the boat and tossing them into the bucket of water that would keep them alive until we got back to the camp. When the giant buckets were overflowing and everyone in the boat could reel no more, it was time for Dad to crank up the outboard and head homeward.

Once on shore, we all helped to schlep the pails of groggy fish to the cleaning table where Dad and Jesse would, at last, put the poor creatures out of their misery. After a merciful bop on the noggin, a very sharp knife was used to cut off the head and to remove the fillets from either side of the fish. Do this, times fifty or sixty and it was time to transport the day's catch to the kitchen, where Mother was at the ready.

A relic of a cast iron fry pan was doused with vegetable oil and a generous blob of butter before being placed on the Coleman stove. A sheet of wax paper was spread across the wooden counter where a cup of flour, salt and pepper and a pinch of paprika were married into the perfect dusting for the tender fillets.

There was an assembly line of sorts. Plate of just cleaned fish, flour mixture, hot oil in a fry pan and finally paper towel to drain the golden beauties after a quick flip in the bubbly butter. With barely time for the juicy morsels to get comfy on the counter, they were gobbled down by big hands and little hands alike, still sizzling from their final swim in the hot oil. As fast as Mom could dredge and fry, we were pilfering strips of the delicate perch. Perch so fresh that, mere hours ago, were all swimming in the river unaware of their fate. As another greasy digit hovered over the paper towel, mother let out a yelp, "If you don't stop there will be nothing left for dinner and everyone will have to get back in the boat."

Coming to Visit Tante

Uncle Joe and Tante made their great escape from the Windy City to balmy Lighthouse Point, Florida. After they settled in, bought the obligatory ocean blue rattan furniture for the living room and a barbeque for the screened in back porch, they were ready for some company. Mom and Dad needed little convincing as they packed the station wagon and headed south. Mom was dreaming of a sandy beach, a salty dip and warm tropical breezes and Dad was dreaming about **FISHING**.

Chapter Fifty

We Don't Have to Walk a Mile for our Camel—cigs and being grown up

I have no idea how Nannie and I got on the subject of smoking. Possibly, it was just a coming of age story, like I had with Mother, about getting my period or kissing boys or hanging out with the wrong kind of girls.

She shared this story.

It was 1937 and Amelia Earhart's plane was lost over the Pacific Ocean, the airship Hindenburg exploded, the Golden Gate Bridge was officially opened, Margaret Mitchell won a Pulitzer Prize for "Gone With the Wind", Charlie Chaplin's talkie "Modern Times" was released and there was Adolf Hitler, Franklin Roosevelt and Joseph Stalin.

My aunt, Tante was nineteen years old, living at home on Herrick Street and attending Elmira College. It was a typical evening. The radio was providing background as Pa sat in his easy chair reading his newspaper. Mom was sitting on the floor perusing what her father had already read. She was curious about a cigarette advertisement that was sprawled across one of the pages. She had heard about Camel cigarettes before, on the radio, where the announcer had proclaimed, "I'd walk a mile for a Camel." Now, a newspaper ad had caught her eye. There, larger than life, was a picture of a burly, kind of cow-pokey guy and a pack of Camel cigarettes.

Neither Nannie nor Pa smoked cigarettes and Mom was quite sure that they would not approve of their daughter doing such a thing. Not to be ignored was the fact that church doctrine forbade it along with the consumption of alcohol. It was not something that a woman from a respectable family would ever consider doing. So one might understand Mother's bewilderment when she found a pack of Camels in her older sister's tweed coat pocket, tucked away in the back of their closet.

Dinner was on the table. Nannie sat on the end nearest the kitchen and Pa sat on the other end. The two sisters sat across from each other. Typically, there was not a lot of chit chat during the evening meal. So when Mother broke the silence by blurting out," WE WON'T HAVE TO WALK A MILE FOR OUR CAMEL", the ensuing silence was as thick as the pork chops on their plates. Like a thermometer with the ruby mercury rising to a boiling point, Tante's face grew redder by the second. Nannie looked up in disbelief, as if she couldn't have just heard this proclamation from her second child. Surely, there must be some mistake. A case of sibling rivalry gone completely amok. She cleared her throat as if to signal to her husband that it was time to stop eating and a family meeting must ensue.

That's where Nannie's story ended. I really didn't want to know the gruesome details. It was all too revealing about the dynamics of my mother's and aunt's relationship and why theirs was a rocky one.

Fast forward twenty years. Growing up in the 1950's and the advent of television, created an aura of acceptance and respectability concerning the smoking of cigarettes. Times were changing, attitudes and social mores were changing.

Our culture was changing and much of this change was due to the influence of the silver screen at the movie theatre and the omnipresent small screen that took center stage in more and more living rooms across the country.

Movies were filled with the Hollywood elite lighting up. Starlets, with slender gold-plated cigarette holders, posed for their handsome leading man to flip open his zippo. Followed by curly rings of smoke that hung in the air, waiting to be blown away with a sultry exhale. Edward R. Murrow always had a cigarette smoldering in an ash tray when he did his nightly news broadcast. Dean Martin crooned into the microphone with cigarette in hand. President Roosevelt enjoyed a good smoke as did Humphrey Bogart and Lauren Bacall, Marlene Dietrich, Bette Davis and the mustached, bespectacled Groucho Marx, who was never without a cigar clinched between his teeth.

Smoking was glamorous. Smoking was sexy. Smoking was romantic. Everybody smoked; my parents, my aunt, all of my mother's and father's friends. Everybody. Having a cup of coffee and a cigarette was the way that many Americans started their day and the perfect ending was a cocktail and a smoke. At our house, it was a Manhattan for my Mother and a rye and soda for my Dad, accompanied by a couple of Lucky Strikes.

I would sit on the couch as my parents relived their day; a policy that Dad had to deliver, a trip to the meat market in Burdett, a phone call from a friend in Elmira, business stuff and house stuff and kid stuff. In my mind, they were just as glamorous as Humphry Bogart and Lauren Bacall, sipping and puffing, talking and laughing, making plans for a spaghetti dinner with our neighbors, for a round of golf on Saturday morning, and throwing a cocktail party to kick off Dad's run for councilman for the Town of Dix.

You could be assured that there would be an errant pack of cigarettes left behind and it was on just such an occasion that my curiosity got the best of me. I covertly slipped the cigarettes and a pack of matches off the coffee table and into my sweater pocket. But then what? Surely someone might notice the bulge. I had to get rid of them quickly. I knew if my parents found out, I would be in big trouble. I couldn't tell my sister. She would run straight to Mother. I was reminded of the story that Nannie told me about walking a mile for a camel. Eureka! I had a brilliant solution! I would hide them in a tin box in my bedroom and I would go upstairs straight away before I was found out.

At eight o'clock, my assigned bedtime, I kissed my parents goodnight and climbed the stairs. I passed my sister's room and she was all curled up, purring like a little kitten. Once in my room, I changed into my pajamas in the dark and when I was sure that it was safe, I pulled the pack out of the tin and pried one of the cigarettes out for closer examination. I pressed the tobacco filled, paper covered cylinder close to my nose and sucked in its aroma. Is it possible that it could taste as good as it smelled?

There was only one way to find out. I pushed open my bedroom window, put the cigarette in my mouth and opened the book of matches. Now I knew how to light a match. I had lit plenty of bonfires in Girl Scouts and I was always a bit of a pyromaniac. Actually, once I was grounded for a month for setting a box of Christmas decorations on fire in the garage. But that's another story.

I pulled off the first match, dragged it across the bottom of the matchbook and to my amazement it burst into flames, lighting up my room as if someone had just turned on the light. In my excitement, fear, panic, I lost all focus of what I was doing and as the fire reached the tip of my finger, I let out a squeal and tossed the match on the floor.

I did better on the next match, holding it closer to the end of the cigarette. When the flame touched the tobacco all I had to do was suck in with all my might. How hard could it be? I sucked in with all my might. My mouth filled up with smoke. My lungs filled up with smoke. My nose filled up with smoke. My throat was burning, and I couldn't breathe. My whole world was spinning out of control and now I was about to throw up. I guess I'll have to wait a little longer to grow up.

And grow up I did. The next summer I was invited to go on a trip with my friend Jackie. Her parents were planning a road trip to Pennsylvania to visit her grandmother and I was anxious to tag along. Jackie's grandmother lived in a tiny hamlet that clung to the side of the steep pine covered Appalachian Mountains. Hers was a tiny clapboard house in a row of tiny clapboard houses. It was painted so many years ago that the blue was hardly blue at all. The front porch had a few loose boards, a few missing boards and it listed like an old sailboat on a windy day.

There was a chicken coop in the side yard and a vegetable garden with zucchini vines and pumpkin vines that curled around a trellis. In the morning, we would be sent out to retrieve fresh eggs for breakfast.

What an adventure! This was, hands down, my favorite thing to do. I loved the smell, a sweet combination of straw and sunshine with more than a whiff of chicken poop. In order to accomplish our mission, we had to be cunning. We had to have a battle plan. These hens were not going to relinquish their eggs without some feathers flying.

We tiptoed up to the crates that were stacked three high and gently slid our hand down between the chicken and her straw bed. Slowly, we searched for something warm, something oval, something hard. An egg, to be precise. And with the same deliberate intent, removed said egg and made our great escape, before being pecked to death by an angry bird.

Then there was my second favorite thing to do. Down the street and around the corner was the neighborhood grocery store. A small space with a rickety screen door and shelves and shelves all stacked with stuff. The perfect place to pick up a quart of milk, a loaf of bread or for two naughty teenagers, a pack of cigarettes. Jackie had obviously done this before and assured me that if she told the clerk, who was most definitely not the smartest grape in the bunch, that she was sent on an errand to purchase a box of Vanity Fairs for her mother and if we handed over twenty five cents, these slender pink beauties would be ours.

We hurried out of the store, too afraid to look back. We ran behind the building and down a steep bank of milkweed and thistle, slipping and sliding until we reached the bottom. We continued to run, still not looking back, beads of sweat and gasping for air. At last, we reached an old dilapidated shack wedged between a hill and a giant oak tree. Brush and bramble provided the safe haven that we needed. It was there that I learned how to inhale. How to suck in the hot vapors without choking. Yes, my head was still spinning but this time it was pure pleasure.

I returned home with a souvenir stowed in the side pocket of my suitcase, buried underneath some rolled up socks and underwear. Again, I had to find a place to hide them. An offense such as this and I would be grounded until I graduated from high school. My friendship with Jackie would be terminated without notice, end of story.

Friday night in the summer meant skating at the roller rink at Lakeside Park. In a small town, your entertainment options were limited, and I really liked to roller skate.

For Christmas, Nannie had gotten me white, lace up the front skates with red and white pompoms. No longer did I have to stand in line with the common folk, waiting for the attendant to pull a dusty pair of size sixes from the shelf. No longer did I have to slide my feet into the odorous innards that were so well worn by the masses. The thought that my feet had shared the same skates with stinky feet, feet that were plagued with fungus and toe jam, feet that needed a good scrubbing and a visit from an orange stick and a sharp pair of nail clippers, caused me to shiver all over. Thank goodness that I no longer had to suffer these indignities.

I plopped down on the wooden bench at the entrance and pulled my skates from their metal case. The piped calliope-like music was already blasting from the loudspeaker above my head and there were already a few people circling around and around on the glossy wood floor.

I quietly glided onto the rink and joined the others in the most unobtrusive way. It was as if everyone had their own space, their own slot with no eye contact, no interaction. It was as if I was the only one there. It should not be surprising that I barely noticed that the rink was getting more and more crowded.

There were children clinging to their parents, their little legs unable to control the wheeled monsters that were determined to ruin their fun. Friends from school skated by and occasionally a boy would cruise up behind me and we would skate together for a while.

Then there was the hokey pokey; you put your right foot in, you put your right foot out, you put your right foot in and you shake it all about. And the Whip, where everyone would hold onto the waist of the person in front of them, creating a roller-skating serpent, much like one of those dragons in a Chinese New Year's parade. As the music got faster and faster, the person in the front would skate faster and faster and everyone else would follow. The poor souls, on the end, had to hold on for dear life and pray that they didn't lose their grip and escape Earth's gravitational pull.

At last, I spotted my friend Jackie, who had told me that she would meet me at the roller rink that night. Our plan was not so much about roller skating as it was about smoking cigarettes. She had also managed to smuggle a pack of Vanity Fairs home with her, buried in the bottom of her suitcase. Emboldened by our escapade in Pennsylvania, we had decided to sneak out back when it got dark and light one up.

We were blessed with a moonless night and a bench behind the bathrooms that would provide the perfect cover. We pulled the pink beauties from the pack, struck a match and puffed away. We had not noticed my mother's car pull into the parking lot. We had not noticed my mother speaking to the attendant. We had not noticed my mother walking across the lawn toward the bathrooms. There was no conversation, no condemnation, no defense, no trial, nor rebuttal. The verdict was guilty of smoking behind my mother's back. "Off with her head!"

I didn't see Jackie again that summer. As a matter of fact, I didn't see anyone at all until school started in September. I sat in my bedroom window and watched the neighborhood kids play hide and seek, watched lightening bugs flitter in the bushes next to the house, watched the day turn to night, watched the streetlights flicker on.

Boring.

Chapter Fifty-one

Mother's Plan for The Summer—there was talk of camp

Mother had decided that my summer vacation needed to be more constructive, more monitored, more disciplined. The previous summer, with too much time on my hands and not enough supervision, I had not made good choices. Or to paraphrase...you're a bad kid who cannot be trusted and so your father and I have decided to send you to sleep away camp.

Now, many of my friends went to camp and they professed to really enjoy themselves. Good for them. I was just not one of them. You see, I hated camp. I hated everything about camp, especially sleep away camp.

On the dreaded morning, I made one last final plea for clemency to my father but to no avail. The die was cast. Mother had spoken. My duffle bag was packed; towel, bathing suit, water shoes, sneakers, pajamas, bug spray, shorts and shirts, a sweatshirt for the chilly nights, toothbrush and a Swiss Army knife that Dad had gotten for me from Posse's Five and Ten. Both the duffle bag and my sleeping bag had been, unceremoniously, tossed into the back of the station wagon. I climbed into the backseat and sat without an utterance, a prisoner being taken to the gallows, as my parents and I made the twenty-minute trek to Hidden Valley 4H camp. Though it was but a stone's throw from home, it might as well had been in the wild jungles of Borneo. As the name denotes, it was completely isolated from all civilization. Thank goodness that Nannie had taken pity on me and given me a couple of nickels for my only link to the outside world, a pay phone attached to a pine post outside the mess hall.

We were greeted at the gate by a much too cheery counselor who assured my parents that she would take me under her wing. She gushed that camp would be a wonderful opportunity for me to explore nature, meet new friends, participate in arts and crafts projects, and to earn my junior lifesaving certification. To be honest, I was less than confident that all this blah-blah would ever come to fruition, but my parents surely bought into it hook, line and sinker. Before I knew what was happening, they were both patting me on the head and nudging me toward the bunkhouse. The last I saw of them; they were scurrying off across the parking lot toward the car. I was doomed.

When I got to the bunkhouse, I remembered one of the reasons why I really hated camp. The smell. It was a combination of an old wooden building, an old mattress and an old pair of sneakers that had been left under one of the cots. It was a mix of mildew, mold, dust, dampness and thankfully, a whiff of pine.

Welcome to camp. I unrolled my sleeping bag and tossed it on a bottom bunk in the corner and started to unpack my things, shorts, shirts, undies, socks. I tucked my pajamas under my softie pillow and placed my toothbrush, hairbrush, toothpaste, and hair clips on a rickety nightstand next to my bed.

At the bottom of my duffle bag, was what I was really looking for. Now mind you, when my parents signed me up for camp, they were given a printout of all the things that I would need and a similar list of all the things that were verboten.

Paramount on the no list was "NO FOOD!" No food? Are they kidding? The thought of eating even one meal in the mess hall was unthinkable. But an entire two weeks without my mother's cooking, impossible! An entire fortnight without my grandmother's baking, unbearable!

Fortunately, my grandmother had come to my rescue. My guardian angel had been looking out for me when I discovered, in my now near empty bag, wrapped in a couple of Nannie's old dish towels, a slab of chocolate fudge brownies. My grandmother had smuggled them into my duffle bag when my parents were not looking. It was one of those "don't ask, don't tell" moments. The bottom drawer of the nightstand was empty and would be the perfect hiding place.

That night, after doing battle with soggy mashed potatoes, cold peas and some mystery meat that was masquerading as meat loaf, I made my way to the pow-wow area where everyone was assembling for the nightly singalong and a roaring bonfire. I was told to find a stick and with my Swiss Army knife, I whittled the end to make the perfect point. Marshmallows were passed out and without any further instruction, the stick and glob of sugary confection met the fire and that's where the phrase "happy camper" originated.

When everyone was full of toasted marshmallows and could sing no more campfire songs, it was time to end our day by taking down the Stars and Stripes while one of the counselors tooted taps on a tarnished old well-worn bugle.

I made my way back to the bunkhouse, trailing behind some kids that seemed to know where they were going, found my bunk and pulled my pajamas out from under my pillow. I stalled just long enough until all the lights had been turned out and everyone was all snuggy in their sleeping bags. It was only then that I quickly slipped out of my shorts and shirt and into my night clothes.

I was reminded of another reason that I hated camp…. its total lack of privacy. Gang showers, of which I was terrified of, were looming in the days to come. I'd have to think of something terribly clever to escape them and realistically, could I not shower for the next thirteen days? I'd just have to figure all of this out in the morning.

I was exhausted. I wiggled into my sleeping bag, closed my eyes and tried to assure myself that camp was not all that bad. Almost as soon as I had gotten comfy, my stomach began to grumble and groan. I guess it was just very unhappy about the absence of a proper dinner and a belly full of charred sugary fluff. The growling was so deafening that I was convinced that if I didn't do something quickly, the other campers would be roused from sleep. But what?

It was then that I remembered the chocolate brownies stashed away in my nightstand. I fumbled in the dark until I felt the dish towel covered rectangle and my Swiss Army knife.

Now Dad had given me a quick tutorial on the do's and don'ts of using a pocketknife. It's very sharp, use caution when opening, pay attention to what you're doing, it's not a toy, and always cut away from your hand.

It seemed that I remembered the first four caveats, but number five proved to be problematic. It was understandable that in the pitch dark and in my panicked state, I forgot to cut away from my hand. It all happened so fast. One moment I was salivating over the prospect of munching on something chocolatey and the next I felt a sharp pain like a really bad paper cut and then a gushing of warm liquid that I was quite sure was blood....my blood.

I had never been a terribly squeamish sissy girl, but I was in a strange place, my mother was not sleeping in the bedroom next to mine and I was bleeding. I reached for my shirt on the floor and wrapped it around my finger so tightly that I could feel my heartbeat pulsing in the tip. Soon it would stop and by morning I would feign a scratch and ask for a band aid. And that's exactly what I did.

After breakfast, which was also yucky (I mean, honestly, how can you mess up fried eggs and sausage) it was off to arts and crafts. There was a long picnic table covered with an oil cloth table covering. There was a station set up for each camper with everything that one would need for an exciting morning of boondoggle.

I hurried to the station that had yellow and lime green strips of plastic ribbon (my favorite colors). A helpful counselor got everyone started and then it was just a matter of how long you were willing to weave the spaghetti-like plastic strips together.

I found that my commitment to boondoggle was boundless. There was no limit to the length of time that I would spend, sitting on an old tree stump at the edge of a clearing. Nope, I was happy as a little clam, all by myself, perched Indian style, minding my own business and counting down the days. When I was finished, I would have boondoggle key chains to present to everyone in my family.

I was really trying to make the best of my situation and to be honest, I thought things were going quite well. Quite well until the morning of the third day when we were all lined up like prisoners in a chain gang and marched to the swimming hole for the beginning of our Red Cross Jr. lifesaving training.

It was there that a very serious looking muscle-bound counselor—with sunglasses, a smear of zinc oxide ointment on her nose, a large whistle hanging around her neck, legs apart and hands on hips—barked at the row of shivering neophytes. I'm not sure if I was shaking from the cold dampness of the hour or sheer terror for what I perceived to be a dreadful morning. As I looked around, it was obvious that I was the youngest kid there, the skinniest kid there, the shortest kid there and I was not all that great of a swimmer.

Of course, my own mother hadn't cared about any of that. What if I was four years younger than the others? What if I was scrawny and boney and a crappy swimmer? She was home and I was here, standing with my toes curled around the edge of an algae covered platform.

At the count of three everyone was ordered to dive into the icy cold abyss. Daylight became night, dry became wet and a single splash of water gave away my point of entry.

And then there were bubbles. As I plunged toward the bottom of the pool thousands of bubbles rushed by me, some bursting in the tangles of my hair, some rushing up my nose, some pushed into my slightly parted lips as I grappled with the notion that I was, indeed, out of my element.

I wish that I could put all fears to rest that the next day was less traumatic, but unfortunately, it was not. Nor was the next day or the day after that. All this misery culminated with the final trials that took place on my last day at Hidden Valley.

On this day we had to swim twenty laps, retrieve a five-pound boulder from the bottom and bring it to the surface. And finally, a simulated rescue. I prayed that I would not have to rescue the muscle-bound counselor but when my name was called, the behemoth in a bathing suit was in the water flailing her arms and calling for help. Undaunted, I jumped in and swam confidently toward her, concentrating only on the task at hand. Repeating in my head everything that I had been taught.

I swam around her like a shark circling a shipwreck, looking for some sign of vulnerability, trying to find her weak spot, but she did not have one. In the end, the plan became a full-frontal attack, just "throw your arm across her chest and be done with it" strategy. There was only one tiny problem, there was no way that my arm could reach across her expansive chest. When I tried, and I tried many times, she would simply flip over and shove my head under water. Over and over again until I finally heard the whistle blow and I sulked back to the shore. Fortunately, I was spared some of the humiliation as most of the other campers had returned to the bunkhouse to pack their belongings.

That night at the award ceremony, parents all bristling with pride and expectations, sat on folding chairs in the mess hall waiting for their children to be recognized for their accomplishments. There were awards for best charcoal drawing, best foul shooter, best lean-to builder and of course, Red Cross Jr. lifesaving certificates.

I didn't get any of those, but I did get recognized for my skills at arts and crafts and my dedication to the art of boondoggle.

Chapter Fifty-two
If I Catch it I Can Keep It—determination pays off

When Mom was a little girl, she had a pet rabbit named Mopsy who lived in a hutch on the back porch on Herrick Street. Mopsy was a beautiful creature with soft white fur, pointy, pink lined ears, a cotton ball of a tail and eyes the color of pink jelly beans.

She was the namesake of a character, in one of Nannie's favorite stories, written by Beatrix Potter and the cousin of Peter Rabbit, a fictional character that first appeared in print in 1902. Mother told me many stories about her own adventures with Mopsy. How she loved to spread an old blanket on the grass in the backyard on warm summer days and play tea party with her bunny companion. Nannie would make cream cheese and strawberry jelly finger sandwiches for her daughter and carrot strips and apple slices for Mopsy.

Once after listening to the escapades of Mom and her furry friend, I posed the not so surprising question, "Mother, do you think that I might be able to get a rabbit for Easter?" Of course, I promised to clean its hutch every morning before school and to feed it and make sure that it had fresh water and a carrot to nibble. I studied her face, looking for any clue to what her answer might be and although it wasn't a yes, it also wasn't a no. I was cautiously optimistic and would not overplay my hand by pestering her. I would just have to wait a couple weeks and see what the Easter bunny had in mind.

My mother loved to decorate the house for all the holidays. There were colored lights and boughs of pine wrapped around the front porch railing for Christmas, white sheet ghosts flapped in the wind and pumpkins sat on the steps for Halloween and Indian corn hung on the front door at Thanksgiving. Dad would tease mother by saying that she loved decorating so much that he wouldn't be surprised if she found a life size replica of Punxsutawney Phil and plunked it in the side yard on Ground Hogs Day. Yes indeed, mom loved the holidays and Easter was no exception.

We dipped hard boiled eggs in a bath of pastel food coloring and nestled them in a bed of plastic grass that filled an assortment of large and small woven baskets that Mother had collected over the years.

When I woke up Easter morning, I discovered that the Easter bunny had placed a basket full of candy at the foot of my bed. Nestled inside, were marshmallow peeps and chocolate rabbits, a rainbow of jellybeans and coconut cream eggs.

I tore off the yellow cellophane that stood between me and ecstasy. Before taking my first bite, I took a moment to breathe it all in. The aroma, a mix of cocoa and sugary stuff, coconut and maple, was unmistakable and did not disappoint.

Now it was time to get a move on, after all there was chocolate to be eaten and I had to hustle before Mom temporarily confiscated my basket until I had eaten my breakfast. I had managed to wolf down a handful of jellybeans and bite one of the ears off my chocolate rabbit when I was summoned to the kitchen.

My mother's voice floated up the stairs, "Breakfast is ready. I hope that you are not eating your Easter candy, young lady."

I had just finished the last bite of French toast when I heard Nannie calling from the side door. "Can someone help me with the door? My arms are full." Everyone rushed to the door anxious to help and equally curious about what her arms were full of.

She staggered into the kitchen balancing her pie carrier, and a stack of boxes wrapped in white tissue paper and tied together with pastel colored satin ribbons. Pa was right behind her with a Florsheim shoe box with holes poked all along the sides and top. He signaled to my mother and she nonchalantly motioned in my direction. "Happy Easter", my mother said to me. "Happy Easter", my grandfather echoed as he handed me the box.

My hands were shaking as I peeked under the lid. How beautiful she was, all snowy white and pink. Pink inside her ears. Pink on her nose. Pink eyes like the jellybeans in my Easter basket. She was perfect...the perfect Easter present and I knew right away that I would call her Mopsy.

I was counting down the weeks until the end of school. The days were getting warmer and longer and so I was anxious to get home, finish my homework and after dinner still have time to play outside. At dusk, the street filled up with neighborhood kids looking forward to a game or two of hide and seek. My friend Linda was the first one to be "it". She buried her face into the bark of a century old maple tree and began to count …. thousand one …. thousand two and we all scattered trying to find a place to hide. When she hollered "Ready or not, here I come", it was time to hunker down and stay very still. I had found, what I thought was, the ideal hiding place and I was being as quiet as a little mouse when the oddest thing happened.

A white rabbit went hippity-hoppity right by where I was hiding. If I hadn't been so taken aback, I probably could have reached out and grabbed him. Instead, I screamed, "There's a rabbit in my yard!" and went tearing into the house to tell my parents. To say that they did not share my enthusiasm was an understatement. Instead they told me that it belongs to someone and no, I couldn't keep it. I didn't give up. I continued to plead and beg, beseech, implore and plead some more until Dad could no longer take it. He acquiesced with one condition. I had to catch the rabbit myself. Neither he nor my mother were going to be of any assistance. If I could catch it, I could keep it. Deal.

I made my way to the front yard without even a glimmer of a plan of how I intended to catch this rascally rabbit, but it was going to happen.

Plan A was soon exhausted, literally, as I chased the bunny around and around the yard. Up the hill, across Mom's garden filled with rose-colored peony bushes, down the hill and along the edge of the shrubs that lined the fence on the west side of the property. This little critter was fast,

251

lightning fast and he could turn on a dime. The hare and tortoise fable came to mind.

As I squatted in the bushes trying to catch my breath, content to only watch from the sidelines, it became quite clear that although this rabbit was nimble and agile and turbo charged, I had discovered his Achilles heel. His route never changed. He always went up the hill, across Mom's garden, down the hill and along the edge of the shrubs.

It was from this observation that plan B was born. I would simply crawl under the shrubs and lie real still until he hopped by and then I would pounce. I watched and waited and waited and waited. I watched him nibble on some dandelion greens, hop down the hill, sniff some dirt in the flower bed, hop some more.

By now it was dark, very, very dark and I could barely see him. I knew that I was running out of time and that any minute Mom was going to call me into the house and who knows where my rabbit might be in the morning.

Then by some miracle something spooked him, maybe it was Sheppie barking, and he tore by me in route to his great escape. I thrust both of my arms out of their hiding place and grabbed at air and dirt and grass and rabbit. I felt something furry. I felt something wiggly. I had caught the elusive bunny. He was mine. Triumphantly, I trudged up the hill and into the house to proudly announce that victory was mine. Mom and Dad didn't seem all that surprised.

After all, I was the little girl with a mind of her own.

Chapter Fifty-three
The Smell of Smoke—quick reactions

The house was asleep. Sheppie was curled up at the foot of Mother's bed. The cat had been put out hours ago for a night of hunting. Everyone was wrapped in darkness and drifting into dreaminess. Everyone except my father.

He had gotten home late after a long night of meetings and politics. His friend, Richard, had followed him home and the plan was to unwind with a night cap and more talk. Dad pulled a bottle of Seagram's Seven from the liquor cabinet, filled two highball glasses with ice, added the whiskey and a splash of club soda and joined his friend at the kitchen table.

He and Richard had been friends for a very long time and that was not at all surprising as they were like minded in so many ways. They were both business owners and that gave them much commonality. They were both Republicans believing in less government. Both were quite conservative, pull yourself up by your bootstraps conservatives, John Wayne was their hero kind of conservatives, with a heavy dose of the Protestant work ethic and male dominance all wrapped up in an adorable way. All of this happened with little ego or pretense. They laughed easily and often, loved a good game of gin rummy at the Elks Club and played golf, lots and lots of golf.

On this particular night, the main topic of rehashing was my father's campaign for town councilman. Much had to be planned and there would be many late nights like this one before election night in November. They hammered out a schedule of lodge meetings, a Chamber of Commerce breakfast, a drop-by at local businesses and a cocktail party idea that he had to run by Mother.

Pleased with what they had accomplished and agreeing that the rest could wait, they called it a night. Dad walked his friend to the kitchen door where the stillness of the hour had taken on a strange hue. The darkness had been tainted with a gray haziness and the unmistakable smell of smoke.

The two men raced up the hill to the street behind our house so that they might catch sight of whatever was burning. They looked no farther than the house next door. The house of John and Betty Spanos, who were dear friends of my parents.

There was no question that the entire first floor of the house was engulfed with flames. Fire shot out of window openings that had exploded from the intense heat. Red hot tongues scorched the outside of the structure as the interior roared even redder.

The siren from the fire station at the end of Decatur Street had begun to summon the volunteer firemen to exit their warm beds and race to the station. There they would jump into their gear and then into the singular village fire truck and proceed to whatever emergency laid ahead.

My father knew that there was no time to waste. He knew that his friends were trapped in the upstairs bedroom and he knew that the only way that they might be saved was to somehow get a ladder and enter the house through the bedroom window.

There would be no waiting for the firemen, by the time they arrived it might be too late. They had no other choice but to get the ladder from the basement and proceed with their plan. They carried the ladder across the backyard and leaned it up against the side of the garage. The garage roof connected to the main house right where the Spanos were sleeping.

Thankfully, before they started to climb up the ladder, the fire truck pulled up in front of the house. With lights flashing and the siren blaring, the firemen emptied out of the truck and flew into action. Hoses snaked to the hydrant in front of Mrs. White's house and began to soak what was once the kitchen and living room. Firefighters made their way to the carport roof and with a pickax smashed the glass in the bedroom window. An enormous cloud of black smoke rolled out like an angry cumulonimbus trapped where it didn't want to be. The firemen entered as Dad and Richard watched from the ground. Their eyes transfixed, they waited for any sign. Any sign of their friends.

At last, they got a glimpse of something moving inside the dark space. There was a fireman carrying a woman and then a man in pajamas and the second fireman. They clamored off the roof, down the ladder until they reached the ground. Our neighbors were covered with ash and gasping for air but after being checked out by the paramedics, it was announced that they would be just fine.

Chapter Fifty-four

Learning the Hard Way—what's right, what's wrong

There was no grey area, no room for interpretation, in the way my Mother and Father parented. I was raised with a rather narrow, rigid definition of right and wrong. Many times, their explanations took on biblical significance. "Do unto others as you would have others do unto you" springs to mind. Another that was often used when my bedroom was particularly messy, "Cleanliness is next to Godliness." Or translated, "don't come out of your room until your bed is made and all of those clothes are either hung up, folded, put in your dresser or in your laundry hamper."

My Nannie was notorious for such Irish inspired blarney as "You lie down with the dogs and you rise with their fleas" when she was not pleased with my choice of friends. If I did not take the hint, she was quick to spout, "You can't make a silk purse out of a sow's ear." Not so subtle.

And let's not forget The Ten Commandments, where I was reminded to honor my mother and father and that it was a sin to tell a lie. Likewise, it was a sin to take what was not yours. Unfortunately, it was the latter where I stumbled.

There was a five and dime store called Posse's on the main street where I would roam the aisles whenever I had some birthday or holiday money burning a hole in my pocket. Posse's had everything. There was jewelry with rhinestones and fake pearls and gold that made a greenish brown ring on your wrist if you wore it more than a day. There were pots and pans and dishes, silverware, can openers and toasters. There were lamps and café curtains for the kitchen and towels in a rainbow of colors and shower curtains for the bathroom. There were racks of clothes and piles of shoes and a table stacked high with denim jeans. There were sweaters and heavy winter jackets, on the mark down rack, in the back of the store.

And there was a pink cinch belt.

It all happened innocently enough. I was trolling the ladies' accessories aisle, between the handbags and hosiery, when something caught my eye. Like a beacon in a fog of browns and blacks, was the most beautiful cinch belt that I had ever laid my eyes on. It was the color of pink carnations, of pink clouds at sunset, of pink cotton candy, of pink rose buds. It was made with a satin material with a gold clasp adorned with three iridescent faux pearls.

When I saw that Mr. Posse was busy behind the cash register, I decided to take it down from the display rack for a closer look. What would be the harm if I just wrapped it around my waist? For a minute... just a minute...and then I would put it right back where I found it. No one would know. No one would see me.

As luck would have it, the cinch belt was way too big but if I tied a knot in the back, it was perfect. Perfect, at least, from the front. I remembered that there was a mirror in the ladies dressing room and I couldn't resist taking a peek. As I twirled in front of the mirror, I couldn't take my eyes off the beautiful piece of pinkness that I had somehow taken ownership of.

I quietly left the store, my heart pounding and my legs shaking. I feared that any moment I would get a tap on the shoulder, be taken off to jail, never to see my family again.

To my relief, I was not tapped on the shoulder nor was I dragged off to jail. I was actually walking up the hill toward my house with the pink cinch belt still around my waist. I hurried up the steps to the front porch, opened the front door, hurried by my father's office and up the stairs to my bedroom.

I quietly shut the door behind me. By now, I was panting like Sheppie on a hot summer's day. At first, I thought it was because I had been in such a hurry to get away from the store. But all too soon, I realized that I had done something very, very bad. Something that I knew would really disappoint my parents if they found out. And my friends? What if they found out? And my teachers? And my Nannie and Pa? I'd bring such humiliation and shame to my family that they would have no choice but to ship me off to boarding school, which was a great deal like prison but it cost a whole lot of money.

I paced back and forth, feeling hot from head to toe, feeling that at any moment I was going to throw up, feeling guilty, wanting to cry. And the cinch belt, the stupid cinch belt, I really hated it. I never wanted to see it again. For now, I would hide it under my mattress and figure this whole mess out later.

There was dinner and homework and some television to watch and I was thankful that I had somehow forgotten about what was lurking under my mattress. It all came flooding back as soon as I climbed into my bed that night. I tossed and I turned, covered my head with my pillow, kicked off all the blankets, but it was no use. I could not get comfortable. I felt like the princess and the pea and the pea was a pink cinch belt. In desperation, I pulled it from its hiding place, opened my bedroom window and flung it into the darkness with all my might. Finally, I could sleep.

In the morning, the pink cinch belt episode seemed like a terrible nightmare and I was sure that there was no other logical explanation. It was a bad dream and today everything was going to be fine. Fine until I looked out of my bedroom window and saw the pink cinch belt draped over the forsythia bush under my bedroom window. Panic returned with a vengeance.

Dire circumstances call for extreme measures. I would sneak into the cellar and get one of mother's garden shovels and I would dig a hole under the forsythia bush and I would bury the pink cinch belt so I would never, ever lay eyes on it again.

Lesson learned.

Chapter Fifty-five
Bad Dreams—but what do they mean

There were two recurring nightmares. Nightmares that I never told anyone about. Bad, bad dreams that wouldn't go away. Scary dreams in black and white and terrifying dreams in Technicolor. Nightmares so real that I would wake with streams of sweat that dripped from the top of my head, welled up in the hollows under my eyes, down over my cheeks, wetting my hair and soaking my pillow. Nightmares so real that at bedtime, I was afraid to close my eyes. Afraid that the dream would come back.

The first dream was on Herrick Street, my grandparents' house. Nannie and I were alone in the dining room. It was getting dark outside, the sun had set and evening was making its presence known. Likewise, inside the house, a grayness filled the rooms and begged for someone to turn on a light. We were always standing in a ghostlike fog.

Nannie would only be wearing her corset that was laced up the front, garters for her stockings dangled from the bottom edge and giant silky underpants. And that was all.

We would be standing around the dining room table when I would hear just the faintest of sounds. My stomach would knot, and bile would rise in my throat. I would listen. We would both listen, our eyelids stretched open so wide that the roundness of our eyeballs was obvious. I knew right away what the sound was. There was a steady drumbeat, bum...bum...bum...bum and it was getting louder and louder and closer and closer.

A band of renegade Indians were marching ten abreast down the center of the street, their moccasined feet barely making a sound and they were headed our way. I coaxed my grandmother down the cellar stairs. We would hide in the dark dankness hoping that they would not find us. Hoping not to be dragged off and butchered by the marauding savages. We huddled behind stacks of bushel baskets filled with potatoes and rutabaga, trying to stay so quiet, so still.

The beating of the drums was now deafening. I clasped my hands over my ears, praying that they would pass by our house, hoping that some other young girl and her grandmother would be their victims. Alas, the drumming stopped and only the soft whispers of the raiding party could be heard. Murmurings in some strange Iroquois tongue and the shuffling of leather soles, first on the front steps, then whispering across the porch.

The front door creaked trying to warn us that strangers were now inside. Inside the vestibule, down the hallway and into the dining room. From our hiding place, I could see the slightest bead of light that streamed from the now opened cellar door. I could see them, war paint smeared across their prominent noses. I could hear them as they crept down the stairs. I could even smell them as a mix of sweat and horse sucked up the air that I was struggling to breath.

Dream number two was quite different, quite short but equally terrifying. I was trudging up the hill in front of our house after a nondescript day at Watkins High. My eyes were downcast, studying the all too familiar imperfections in the blocks of concrete. Trying to avoid stepping on the cracks in the sidewalk. "Step on a crack and you'll break your mother's back." I knew I was home when the bottom step of our front porch reached out to the sidewalk. I stood there for a minute to catch my breath, still not bothering to look up. Everything around me was very, very still. Lunar still. Like a vacuum without even a trace of anything to breathe.

In the beginning of this black and white nightmare there was no color, no sound and no smell. Without a moment's notice I was all too aware that something had changed. Something had splattered on my bare legs. It was something warm, something wet, something red. There was a sanguine scarlet dampness that stained my skin, my plaid wool skirt and the tops of my penny loafers.

With exaggerated timidity, ever so slowly, I raised my head and saw that someone hung from a rope that had been meticulously wrapped around and around the metal sign that advertised my father's business. His head jerked to the side, snapped like a duck hanging in the window of a Chinese market. His extremities were a deathlike blue black, his eyeballs bulging in disbelief and his tongue hanging out in one last, final deviant gesture.

I'm sure that there were other dreams, other nightmares that I was more than relieved to awaken from. These two, in particular, stuck in my memory because they recurred all too often, unannounced and certainly unsolicited over the course of many years.

Chapter Fifty-six
A Spoonful of Sugar—never helped the medicine godown

I learned, at a very early age, that there were some things that were just better left unsaid. Things like, I think that I'm getting a cold, or my throat is burny and I'm having a hard time swallowing, or I have a sore on the inside of my bottom lip, or I have an ear ache, or I have a cut on my finger, or I haven't pooped lately.

Of course, there were medicines, elixirs of sort for all these ailments but none of them were particularly pleasant. Wild cherry cough syrup, grape flavored lozenges, peppermint flavored antacids were, but a dream spinning in the head of some young chemist toiling in a lab of some pharmaceutical company.

Our medicine cabinet was jammed full of bottles and jars and tins that contained tonics and ointments reminiscent of the concoctions that were once peddled from the wagons of unscrupulous snake oil salesmen.

If I complained of chest congestion or had a bad cough, Mother would conjure up a mustard plaster, a poultice of mustard seed powder in an unsavory emulsion, which was smeared inside a large swath of cheese cloth and placed on my chest. It was then secured by wrapping yards and yards of gauze around my torso until I looked like a mummy being readied for the tomb.

A sore throat was no match for a teaspoon of Tonsiline which came in a rectangular shaped glass bottle. The bottle was embossed with the head and neck of a giraffe, symbolizing the effectiveness of the contents. It's a challenge, at best, to describe just exactly what Tonsiline tasted like, but its putrid chartreuse hue was an indication of what was to come. It was a cross between gasoline and paint thinner with a shot of sulfuric acid. It was so bitter that at contact with a single taste bud, my tongue would swell, my cheeks and lips would pucker, tears would stream from my eyes and an uncontrollable shudder would leave me shaking like a leaf. As proof of its noxious potency, it actually turned one of mother's spoons from a silver patina to the greeny-black color of mucky swamp water. Of course, I questioned Mother about this, but she never was terribly forthcoming in relieving my concerns.

I never, ever mentioned that I had a canker sore until the inside of my mouth looked like it was being gnawed on by a flesh-eating amoeba. When I could no longer stand the pain, it was time for the tin of powdered alum.

Alum is a chemical compound that looks like baking powder. However, its benign appearance belies the stinging, burning sensation that happens when alum meets canker sore. After Mother packed the powder on the affected area, I had to walk around for at least five minutes, with my lip pulled out like a Mursi tribe's woman, so that the alum wouldn't get washed away by the ocean of saliva that filled my mouth.

Also to be found in the medicine cabinet was the indispensable bottle of Merthiolate. This dark red caustic liquid came in a small bottle with a glass wand applicator attached to the cap. If I had a cut or a scrape, any gash or contusion Mom would apply a dab or two of Merthiolate to the affected area and as she swiped the dreaded wand over the sore, she would instruct me to blow…blow…blow on it. And for good reason. It burned like the Dickens!

I hesitate to mention about the dire consequences of not pooping. Mother had a preoccupation with regular bowel movements. One might even consider it an obsession. So if there was a query about the last time I went number two, I knew that it would not be long before the dreaded red rubber enema bag was pulled out of the linen closet and hung like an instrument of torture from the shower nozzle. The premise from this point on seems obvious and the rest will have to be left to one's imagination, as I hesitate to continue with this all too personal and somewhat sordid conversation.

Lastly, there were earaches. It seemed like my younger sister always had one. Every time she had a cold, she got an earache. Every time she went swimming, she got an earache. They were mighty painful. It was not an uncommon occurrence for the entire family to be awakened in the middle of the night by the sobs and howls of my sister clutching her ear.

The remedy for an earache came straight from our Irish ancestors. Mother simply packed an old pipe with Prince Albert tobacco, struck a match and puffed furiously until the contents of the pipe were glowing a purply red and there was plenty of smoke. Mom took long slow drags from the pipe stem and filled her lungs and throat with the warm vapors and proceeded to blow them into the affected ear. This almost always did the trick. The crying ceased, the lights were turned off and everyone was able to get back to sleep.

There was only one time that I can remember that this treatment didn't work. This was when my sister stuck a black crayon in her ear and Mom, after making the discovery, deftly removed it with a pair of her eyebrow tweezers and then fired up the pipe for another try.

There were occasions when our ailments were more serious, not in Mother's bailiwick, and we had to go to the doctor.

There was a time when I had a real, real, real bad sore throat. My lymph glands on the sides of my neck were all swollen and when Mom looked in the back of my throat there was a mass of bloated, blood red, tonsils covered with white pus-filled pocks. The diagnosis was acute tonsillitis and I was scheduled to have my tonsils removed surgically at the Arnot Ogden Hospital the next week.

I was not at all happy about having to have surgery. There was no way that I was going to put on one of those ugly hospital gowns. There was no way that I was going to open wide and let a stranger with a sharp instrument cut my tonsils out of the back of my throat. There was no way that I was going to let someone put a mask over my nose to make me go to sleep. I begged Mom for a double dose of Tonsiline. I would gargle with warm saltwater. Anything was worth a try. My mother was not listening.

It was raining buckets on the fateful morning. An omen that I was sure would determine my chances for survival. What could I do? Mom was not going to budge. It was a long shot, one last ditch effort when I approached my father with my concerns about the hazards of driving all the way to Elmira in such inclement weather. The roads would be slick, visibility could be a problem and fog. There could be fog so thick that we might skid off the road and end up in a ditch. Certainly, we could reschedule for a later date.

He didn't answer right away and when he did, I'm quite certain that I saw the briefest of smirks on Dad's face before he feigned a touch of compassion and directed me to take my concerns to my mother.

The drive to Elmira was uneventful. The rain had let up considerably. It was a mere drizzle and no fog. When we got to the hospital entrance an orderly pushing an empty wheelchair came out and instructed me to hop aboard. I was not impressed with his hospital humor, but I did what he said.

Everything was pretty routine once I got inside. Mom accompanied me into pre-op where I did put on the ugly hospital gown. It wasn't long before the anesthesiologist came in to explain that he was going to put ether, a colorless liquid, on a piece of gauze and place it over my nose. The ether would cause me to go into a very deep sleep. I would be instructed to start counting backwards from one hundred and by the time I got to ninety-five I would be out like a light.

And so it was. I said goodbye to my mother and made her promise that she would not leave the pre-op under any

267

circumstances. Insisting that she cross her heart and hope to die to validate her pledge. The same orderly that had met me in the parking lot pushed me down the hall and through the swinging doors of the operating room. Once inside, I was surprised by the stark blue white light that flooded the room. So bright that I had to close my eyes. And cold. It was very, very cold. Immediately, I began to shiver under the paper-thin cotton sheet that covered me. So cold that my teeth were chattering out of control.

I was not comforted in the slightest when I saw the anesthesiologist approaching and just like he had explained earlier, he put this yucky smelling cloth over my nose and told me to breathe deeply and slowly and to begin to count backwards from one hundred. And so I began. One hundred, ninety-nine, ninety-eight, ninety-seven, ninety-six...I was not asleep.

Eighty-three, eighty-two, eighty-one...I was still not asleep... Without taking his eyes off the monitor, the anesthesiologist voiced his concern to the OR team. What was going on with this patient? Why wasn't this kid succumbing to the effects of the ether? Why was this taking so long? Was she purposely fighting to stay awake? And there was the obvious danger that this much ether could have devastating consequences to their young patient.

Both of the doctors knew my mother. They knew that she was an RN. They knew that she was a graduate of this very hospital. They remembered working with her when she was a surgical nurse on staff. They knew that she was waiting in the wings.

The decision was made to have Mother scrub and come into the operating room, hoping that her presence would bring an end to this nonsense and that there would be a deep sleep and the tonsillectomy would go on without any further complications. That's exactly what happened.

Later that night, huddled in the hallway outside my room, the surgeon spoke quietly to my parents and while he reassured them that all was well, he also mentioned that their daughter was quite strong willed. To which my father replied,

"Yes indeed. That little girl has a mind of her own."

Chapter Fifty-seven
Stores that Lined Franklin Street—almost anything that one might need

Hundred-year-old buildings sat on the main street of my tiny hometown. Buildings that were built with rock hard materials meant to last for generations. Edifices in a potpourri of timeless architectural styles that separated them from the mundane. Buildings that housed the businesses of merchants that serviced the townspeople and those who lived on the farms and homesteads of the adjacent countryside.

The four corners and the only traffic light designated the center of the village. There was the Jefferson Hotel, the Glen National Bank, Gus' ice cream and soda shop, and the A&P food market.

Mother would go to the A&P to do her grocery shopping every Thursday afternoon in preparation for the weekend. Though it sounds a bit silly, a trip to the grocery store was something of a formal affair. There was a rather strict code of dress if you planned on wandering through the aisles of the A&P. Think business attire... silk blouse, slim wool tweed skirt and matching jacket, nylon stockings, high heels, a perfectly quaffed page boy and red lips. Mother never went shopping without her white gloves. Why would anyone wear white gloves to the A&P?

That was just the proper thing to do.

Quite naturally, all my parents' personal and business dealings pertaining to finances were done at the Glen

National Bank, as it was the only bank in town. Everyone at the bank knew all their customers, my parents included. They knew that we lived in the Victorian house just up the hill from the bank, they knew that my father drove a navy blue Ford station wagon, they knew that our family came from Elmira, they knew that my father's mom lived in a trailer park in Sarasota. When Dad walked into the bank it was like old home week. It was comfortable. It was personal.

The Jefferson Hotel was the Grand Dame of the village and the perfect place for my parents to meet friends and chitchat over a couple of cocktails at the bar and dinner in the dining room. It was the perfect place to take special agents from the Travelers Insurance home office for drinks and a chance to unwind after spending an afternoon pouring over policies and premiums and profit and loss ratios. The hotel, built in 1832, had history and charm in abundance. It was the perfect place for both business and pleasure.

I had little interest in any of the aforementioned. I was too young to sit at the bar at the Jeff. I didn't have any money so a trip to the bank would be a waste of time and I hated going grocery shopping.

That leaves Gus' Ice Cream and Soda Shop that occupied the first floor of a beautiful, old, three story Italianate structure on the northwest corner of Franklin and Fourth Street. Inside, little had changed in the decades that the burly old man, originally from Greece, had been scooping up ice cream and pouring melted chocolate magic into metal candy molds. Molds that he had brought here from the old country.

The floor was a well-worn marble that a century ago had been cloud white with ribbons of gray and black, but now after years of wax and wear, it had a rather creamy patina and only the faintest notice of any other color.

The room had a mile-long alabaster marble counter lined with timeworn red leather stools that were begging to be swiveled. Antique glass display cases introduced all who entered an opportunity to experience confection Nirvana.

On the far end of the shop, there were tables and along the wall, there were wooden booths. Their own history was chronicled by generations of young lovers, who clandestinely scratched their initials, encased in crude heart shapes, on the tabletops, as they shared a chocolate ice cream soda and dreamed the dreams of puppy love.

The smell of chocolate permeated the air. An essence that wrapped around you like an old woolen blanket on the first chilly night in autumn. Beyond the tables was a door to the kitchen. There was an extra-large rectangular worktable where at any time of any day, the old man could be found hunched over his molds or sheet pans making chocolate something.

He was especially busy just before the holidays, Christmas, Easter, and Valentine's Day. That's when the display cases told it all. At Christmas, giant chocolate Santas with white icing beards and chocolate sleighs filled with nougats and red and green striped ribbon candy lined the shelves.

My favorite was the chocolate kewpie dolls that came in assorted sizes and all decorated with colorful icing for the eyes and the mouths and a little trim around their necks.

Of course, for Easter, there was a multitude of chocolate bunnies and coconut cream filled eggs and tons and tons of jellybeans. Straw baskets stuffed with green plastic grass were filled to overflowing with one of the enormous bunnies taking center stage in a nest of chocolate eggs and jellybeans.

Valentine's Day was celebrated with chocolates of every shape and flavor gently placed in colorful paper cups and arranged in beautiful red satin heart shaped boxes. So romantic.

However, Gus' Ice Cream Shop was not just about the holidays. On warm summer nights, there was nothing better than the whole family sitting at the counter feasting on root beer floats or cherry cokes or banana splits. Sometimes, Mom would send me with fifty cents to buy a quart of vanilla ice cream that would be drowned in her homemade hot fudge sauce. Then all that was needed was a sprinkling of Spanish peanuts and a Mexican sundae was born.

Yum, yum, yummy.

A close second on my favorites list had to be the bakery which was just a few blocks down the street. Smells of all things baked and delicious trickled through the cracks in the front door and the Pied Piper sweetness beckoned me.

On a cold winter's morning it wasn't just toasty inside, there was an equatorial atmosphere of warmth and yeast and sugar cinnamon. Dumbstruck, I would stand in front of the glass display case. My eyes darting back and forth like I was watching a Chinese ping pong match. Back and forth and up and down until I spotted the cherry pies. In this world, everyone has a food that they just can't get enough of. Maybe it's crispy bacon draining on a piece of greasy paper towel, maybe it's corn on the cob dripping with butter and salt, maybe it's chocolate chip cookies just pulled from the oven, but for me it was cherry pie. Cherry pie with a lattice crust so the lush redness of the fruit inside was able to peak through the top.

I wanted a cherry pie and I didn't want to share it with anyone. I wanted to eat the whole thing. How was that going to happen? First off, it's not like I would be so foolish as to approach my mother with a request for seventy-five cents to buy a pie that I planned on hording in my bedroom. Secondly, she would have thought it a total waste of money to buy a pie when Nannie was the expert pie maker and made pies for free. Probably the most compelling reason after one and two, was that I didn't have any money of my own.

My parents didn't believe in giving children an allowance for doing chores around the house. If I needed money for whatever reason, I simply asked and if they thought that it was a reasonable request and not frivolous, they gave me the money. Somehow, I knew that this query would not fly.

It was time to put on my thinking cap. It was time for some creative financing. Luckily, I remembered that sometimes in the late afternoon, Dad would stretch out on the couch in the living room for a short snooze before dinner. I also remembered that, on occasion, loose change would slip out of his pants pockets and disappear in the cracks between the seat cushions.

I decided that I would make periodic sweeps and collect the errant coins. This seemed like a perfect plan. It was innocent enough, even quite ingenious if you asked me. Not that I thought that I was doing anything wrong, but regardless, I decided that it would be best if I didn't share this with my parents. For the next few weeks, I would forage between the pillows in search of buried treasure until I had the long-awaited cash on hand.

The very next day on my way home from school, I made a slight detour and just happened to find myself standing outside the bakery. I pressed my nose up against the glass sidelight for a better look at the rack of pies that were stacked just inside the door. There it was. The third pie from the top, nestled between a lemon meringue and a blueberry. It was a beauty.

It was time for my game face as I slipped inside, approached the lady behind the counter and nonchalantly made my purchase. I exited quickly with my cherry pie wrapped in white butcher paper and tied with a string. When I started up the hill, I hid the pie in my book bag being very careful not to smoosh it.

I quietly opened the front door and scurried upstairs to my bedroom. My heart was pumping with fear and delight, with anticipation and excitement and with a tad of regret and guilt that I tried to purge from my consciousness. I pulled the pie from my book bag, unwrapped it and placed it on my bed as if it were the crown jewels on display in the Tower of London. What a beauty!

The crust was golden and the filling ruby red. It was shiny from the egg wash and sparkly from the sugar that dusted the pastry top. And smell...the smell was as if I had carried the entire bakery home in my backpack.

I began to fear that Mom might find out what I was up to. What if she walked down the hallway and got a whiff or worse yet, barged into my room with an armful of folded laundry.

I decided to take refuge in the back of my closet. I cleared a space, sat cross-legged in the darkness with the pie in my lap and after realizing that I had forgotten a spoon from the kitchen, pulled a giant piece of pastry from the top. I stuffed the crust into my mouth followed by a finger full of sweet fruit filling. I continued this Great White feeding frenzy until there was an ominous hole where the pie used to be.

I was oblivious to the notion that my tummy had gone from euphoria to Grenoble melt down. It was making the strangest gurgling noises. Sounds that I had never heard before, followed by a series of growls and moans. Yet to come, was a wave of indigestion followed by rollers of nausea and finally a tsunami of vomit.

At dinner that night, I pushed the food around on my plate hoping that it would somehow disappear and when that didn't happen, I asked if I could be excused and went straight to bed.

Chapter Fifty-eight

When Is a Blanket a Tent—and when is a tent just some blankets?

I had tent making in my blood like some kind of Bedouin lineage buried in my DNA. Something that compelled me to look at a blanket, not as a bed cover, but as a potential home for me and my dolls and my stuffed animals.

When I got older, a tent provided me with a cloistered place to read and hang out with whatever unsuspecting family pet wandered by, unfortunate enough to be in the wrong place at the wrong time.

It all started when I was a tyke visiting Nannie on Herrick Street. There were times when my grandmother had things to do other than entertain her rather demanding house guest. After all, there were only so many times that she could walk around the block or swing on the glider on the front porch or pick flowers in the side yard. There were times when she just could not muster another game of old maid or connect the dots or hide and seek.

By four o'clock she really had to begin preparing dinner. Pa would be home soon, and dinner had to be ready. She would pull an old blanket from a shelf on the back porch and toss it over the dining room table.

Voila, a tent was born.

Then came the amenities to make the new space my own. First, I brought two pillows down from Nannie's bed and all my favorite books from the bookcase in the hallway upstairs. Once they were neatly stacked inside my tent, I realized that it was much too dark for reading and I would need a light. I found a small lamp on the desk where Nannie paid bills and luckily, it had a long extension cord attached. An upside-down paper basket made a perfect table for the lamp.

Nannie delivered a tray complete with porcelain teapot with matching cups and saucers, cotton napkins and one of her fancy hand painted china dishes stacked with sugar cookies.

I invited my sister's stuffed French poodle, Fifi, to join me and as the two of us lounged and read stories and sipped and munched, Nannie busied herself whipping up a tuna noodle casserole and a batch of dinner rolls.

At five o'clock, everything had to be put away as the table morphed from tent to table in anticipation of the evening meal.

At home on Lovell Avenue, there were summer tents and winter tents. Those long summer days begged for something to do and Mother preferred that I do that something outside.

A quick trip to Dad's shed on the far end of the property provided a bonanza of materials for building the perfect tent. There was a stack of wooden sawhorses, cinderblocks, bricks, metal clamps and old paint tarps that all had to be dragged to the side yard where a beautiful old apple tree would provide the perfect venue. There would be shade from the low hanging limbs and fruit for munching hung within arm's reach. Accompanying me inside was my faithful dog friend and loyal canine companion Jip, who was only a tad reluctant to spend his days inside a sweltering canvas lean-to. But being the good sport that he was and coaxed with a hot dog that I had smuggled out of the kitchen, he went along with my shenanigans.

One of my favorite things to do in my tent was to play tea party. I had a set of plastic teacups, saucers and a pot in which to make the wildflower tea. I foraged for dried clover blossoms that I smooshed between two bricks. Then it was into my tea pot, covered with water and positioned on my rock stove that I had built just outside the flapped entrance of my tent.

While I waited for the tea to steep, I busied myself by making a batch of sugar cookies. No tea party would be complete without something delectable to dunk in my tea. To make my rather unconventional cookie, I mixed dirt and water in a large bowl. Mom had given me some well-worn utensils, a long-handled metal spoon, measuring cups, an old wooden rolling pin, a cookie sheet, a bag of assorted cookie cutters and I found a small piece of plywood leaning up against the shed that made the ideal worktable. It was there that I rolled out my dough and cut my cookies into a myriad of shapes. From there it was into my brick oven which had been preheated to whatever temperature the sun happened to be and then Jip and I waited. Once out of the oven, I decorated the top of each cookie with delicate flower petals, tiny leaves, pinecone seeds and dried blackberries that I had scavenged from the field next to my house.

I pulled the leftover hot dog from my jacket pocket and with my Swiss Army knife cut a sliver to decorate the top of Jip's cookie which I then put on a plate and placed in front of him. Cautiously he sniffed, before ever so carefully removing the hot dog garnish with his canines. All of this he did without getting a speck of dirt in his mouth.

He was a very intelligent dog indeed.

Chapter Fifty-nine

Teenage Rebellion—finding my spiritual self

When Mom and Dad had set up housekeeping in Elmira, we began attending Sunday services at the German Lutheran Church. This was the same church that my father had attended as a young boy, his mother and father had been parishioners there for years and the presiding minister had married my parents in a lovely outdoor ceremony in Nannie's garden on Herrick Street.

When we moved to Watkins there wasn't a Lutheran Church in town, nor was there one close by, so Mom and Dad decided that the Presbyterian Church might be an acceptable alternative. It turned out to be a perfect fit for my parents.

The church had a large congregation with a solid base of conservative, civic minded businesspeople, a loyal group of elderly parishioners that had been members of the church for years and young families with lots and lots of kids.

After attending Sunday worship for several months, they began taking on some of the leadership roles. They worked on various committees, washed dishes at the Harvest Dinner, Mom gave bread making classes in the church kitchen and Dad gave out bulletins and was an usher at the ten o'clock service. I sang in the youth chorus, on occasion, even though I warbled like a chicken and the rest of the time sat dutifully in the pew with my parents.

I always tried to separate myself from my mother as she had a much stricter code of spiritual etiquette than Dad. But regardless of how I positioned myself I knew that I must sit up straight, ramrod straight, eyes fixed on the pulpit, no fidgeting, no playing with the bulletin, and absolutely no talking, not even a whisper.

Communion consisted of a basket of Sunbeam bread cubes and tiny clear glass cups filled with Welch's grape juice that my father had picked up at the corner market on the way to church. The sermons were particularly grueling as the minister droned on and on and on about biblical stuff for which I had little interest.

As I dressed for church on Sunday mornings, I was partial to my blue and white sundress because it had long navy grosgrain ribbons on the skirt pockets. If I was terribly discreet, I could occupy myself with the heady task of rolling them up so that they resembled tight little rose buds before letting them cascade off my lap. I know that this sounds rather desperate but unfortunately, I was.

When my friend invited me to go to church with her, I was eager to oblige. After all, I was bored to tears most Sundays sitting like a pillar of salt on the unyielding straight-backed pew, my mother hovering about to make sure that I did nothing to embarrass her.

It can't be overlooked that I was a head- strong, willfully willful teenager searching for something and I didn't even know what I was searching for. Searching for some kind of spiritual connection, looking for the path that would take me to a comfortable place where I could talk to God. A place where I could wiggle and whisper and get down on my knees like I did when I would say my prayers with Nannie before hopping into my warm bed on Herrick Street.

A choir of angels greeted me as I stepped inside St. James Episcopal Church for the very first time. Angels that put their wings around me and nestled me next to my friend in a pew at the back of the church. Right away I noticed that the pew was covered with a soft tufted cushion wrapped in well-worn brownish maroon crushed velvet.

The nave was small, almost intimate, in stark contrast to the cold and cavernous churches that I was used to. It was old and a bit musty. It smelled of a hundred years of burning candle wax and once pungent incense. It was dark with just a bit of sunlight trying to push through thick stained-glass windows that created a halo around Jesus and the children that had gathered at his feet.

I had been forewarned that this service, the Holy Eucharist, was nothing like the church services that I was familiar with. It was up and down and up and down. It was up to sing and down to pray. It was up as the cross was carried to the front of the church and everyone bowed their heads and genuflected as they approached the altar for communion. There were kneeling cushions stacked on the floor of each row of pews, so I was on my knees and then on my tush and then on my feet leaving not a moment to be bored or time to be fiddling with some silly ribbon.

The Eucharist was recited from the Book of Common Prayer, parishioners on their knees, heads bowed, eyes closed, and the priest loomed larger than life in his creamy white flowing robe. The front of his vestment was covered with beautifully embroidered symbols of his station and a long satin sash wrapped around his neck and trailed down his torso.

He stood behind the altar with his arms stretched over his head as he held high the communion wafer waiting for God's blessing and then poured wine into a silver chalice repeating the ritual. There was nary a crumb of store-bought bread or a drop of bottled juice to be found. After the blessing, people proceeded single file to the altar railing where they knelt, and a single wafer was placed in the palm of their hands and they sipped wine from the chalice. The priest meticulously wiped the cup with a white napkin after each communal mouthful.

I was absolutely dumbfounded, flabbergasted, speechless. Could this be real? Could this be true? Everyone drinking from the same cup. My girlfriend drinking a sip of wine. Might she feel the effects of the alcohol or feel sick or both?

I knew that my mother would never approve of something so unsanitary. A cup, the perfect petri dish for all things communicable. As I sat soaking up all that I had just experienced, I knew that Mom would not be at all happy with any of it. The kneeling, the crossing of oneself, the priest thing, the giant statue of the Virgin Mary. This was all too much like the Roman Catholic Church that had been the bane for generations of Protestant Orange Irish. It really had little relevance for Mother that the Pope's Catholic Church was blocks away, this church just had too many similarities. Probably the most damning of details, the straw that broke the camel's back, was the fact that it was directly across the street from the Presbyterian Church.

So the mother and the daughter she-bulls blew smoke out of their nostrils, their hooves throwing up clouds of generational dust as they staked their claim, made their point, pleaded and begged and forbade. Horns locked, they argued. Gauntlets were thrown, lines were drawn in the sand, parental privilege was demanded but in the end Nannie came to my rescue and I was allowed to attend services at St James, at least for the short term.

I'm convinced that they were both hopeful that all of this crossing and bowing was just another fleeting phase of a willful, unyielding teenager and that it was far less stressful to just let this run its course than do battle with a sixteen-year-old.

Every Sunday morning, I walked to church. Usually, I would sit with my friend, sometimes I sat all by myself and that was just fine with me. I was there to talk to God. It never got old. It never was boring.

Sometimes I just needed a little pick-me-up midweek and how convenient that there was an abbreviated service every Wednesday morning at seven o'clock. This worked perfectly as I could pop in on my way to school.

I'm reminded of one very dark, very cold, very snowy morning. I left the house wrapped in a wool Navy pea coat, long socks, heavy boots and a knitted scarf that I twisted around and around my neck and then up over my head before I tucked the ends into the top of my jacket. By the time I reached the red wooden doors of St. James, the wind and blowing snow had made it quite clear that they were in a foul mood. I was eager to duck inside to escape the elements.

The candles were ablaze on either side of the altar in the dimly lit sanctuary, and I was suddenly warm. A warm, the likes I had never felt before. It was nothing like the heat that I had felt from a sputtering radiator or a crackling bonfire. It was a liquid warm that poured over me like warm butterscotch sauce atop a double scoop of vanilla ice cream. I knelt in the closest pew and said what I had come to say and then, quickly, found myself out on the sidewalk, heading for school.

And so it was. My mother and father drove to the Presbyterian Church every Sunday with my brother and sister in the back seat of the station wagon and I trudged down the hill to the Episcopal Church.

This all seemed like a perfectly fine arrangement until one Sunday, I got it in my head that I wanted to take my sister and brother to church with me. I approached Dad with the idea, and without even a hiccup, he passed me on to Mother who to my amazement said, "Okay, but please make sure that you hold your sister's and brother's hands when you cross Franklin Street." I assured her that I would hover over them like an old mother hen and raced upstairs to give them the news.

I have to admit that I was feeling terribly grown up when I got my little brother dressed in his white shirt and tartan plaid bow tie and found a lace black mantilla that I bobby-pinned to the top of my sister's head. Off we went.

I had a death grip on their hands from the moment we went out the front door and down the hill. We hurried by the Garden Grill and Shang's Pool Hall, down Fourth Street and then right for just a couple of blocks to the red door.

Once inside, we settled into a pew and I began to frantically show them the ways of the Episcopal Eucharist. During communion, I lead my ducklings to the altar where they knelt, folded their hands like little cherubs and waited for the priest to make the sign of the cross on their foreheads. We made our way back to our pew where we teetered on stacks of cushions to say a prayer of thanksgiving and then one last hymn.

In hindsight, I should have told them that once we got home their only response to Mother's query of "How was church?" should be "It was okay," or something to that effect. Fine, no big deal, anything like that would have worked. But that's not what happened. They never gave Mom a chance to ask the obvious question but instead raced into the house screaming with delight. They chattered away about kneeling on the velvet pads and crossing themselves when they were instructed and genuflecting when they entered or left the pew and last but unfortunately not least, the blessing from the priest.

God forbid.

Chapter Sixty

Coming to Grips with Growing Up—learning how to cope

The PA system chirped three times and everyone in Mr. Donnelly's fifth period World History class swiveled their eyes from their textbook to the tiny square box that was mounted on the wall just above the American flag. There was a second or two of static crackling and then the piercing voice of Miss Murphy, the school secretary.

First off, she apologized for interrupting class. Everyone knew that she interrupted classes all the time, and could have cared less who was learning what, as long as she got her message out. None of this was out of the ordinary. What was unusual, was that I had been summoned to the office and told to bring my coat and whatever else that I might need. I was going home.

I hurried down the hallway making a quick stop at my locker. As I passed the row of windows and approached the office door, I spotted my father standing with the principal, Mr. Moore. What was going on? I tried to reflect on my behavior for the last couple of days and nothing too egregious sprang to mind.

Yes, I had complained to the lunch lady that the soup tasted like dirty dish water and that they really needed to remove the word chicken from the chicken noodle soup menu item because after searching through the entire bowl, there was not a trace of chicken to be found. There was a little bit of a ruckus in Mrs. Smith's Latin II class when Matthew H kept turning around and staring at me. But no big deal.

As I reached for the knob on the office door, Dad excused himself and met me in the hallway. He looked serious. He looked so sad. "Dad, what's going on? What's the matter?" He didn't answer, but instead grabbed my hand and ushered me down the stairs to the side door exit of the school.

Once in the car, he delivered the awful news. Pa had been taken to the hospital during the night and had died that morning. I sat on the front seat, still clutching my coat. Grim-faced, I stared out of the side window, looking at nothing and seeing even less. I was a total stranger to what I was feeling in the pit of my stomach. No one in the family had ever died and my grandfather had not been ill. As a matter of fact, I couldn't remember a time when he had ever been sick, except for an occasional winter cold or a sinus infection. How could he have died so quickly? How could he be gone? And what about Nannie? Who would take care of her, take the car to the garage to get the oil changed, mow the lawn, take the garbage can out to the curb on Thursday? Who would carry her pies from the car into our house on Fourth Street every Thanksgiving?

Fittingly, it was dark, gloomy, with fits of icy sleet, the perfect February day that was good for little else but a funeral. A black hearse led the long line of cars with their headlights conspicuously on high beams as the procession snaked through Woodlawn Cemetery to the family burial plot that had laid fallow for so many years.

I remembered Nannie telling me that one of our relatives was a grave digger in Pennsylvania when he came to this country from Ireland. She told me that he was a muscle-bound brutish man with a quick temper and little humor. I now understood, as I stared out of the tinted window of the limousine at a huge heap of rock and half frozen earth. A pile that was only partially covered by an ugly faux grass green tarp.

We huddled close together and watched as my grandfather was lowered into the hole next to the pile of dirt. The minister said a prayer and it was over.

We made our way back to Herrick Street where Pa's coworkers from the YMCA gathered to remember their friend. They whispered platitudes, told stories and reminisced about what a fine man he had been. They stood in the parlor, in their Sunday best, balancing a glass of punch and cocktail napkin in one hand and a paper plate of tiny finger sandwiches in the other.

Neighbors stopped by to pay their respects and reassured my grandmother that if she needed something, all she had to do was ask. There were relatives that I had never seen before. Total strangers, from Pa's side of the family, that I was introduced to. I said a polite hello and then quickly forgot their names in the sea of faceless faces.

I wandered unnoticed around the cliquish groups of mourners in search of my grandmother. She was nowhere to be found and so I took refuge on the front porch. When I opened the front door, there she was wrapped in her wool tweed winter coat that covered her black gabardine suit, her black pill box hat still perched on the top of her head.

And with broom in hand, she was sweeping the sidewalk in front of the house. This might seem a bit unusual, but it was actually an age-old Irish tradition. When someone died in the family, the sidewalk had to be swept in preparation for the funeral, in preparation for the visitors that would be coming to the house. I assume that this was a throwback to the Irish wake when the house would be overflowing with well-wishers and Irish whiskey.

At long last, everyone was gone. There were sorrowful goodbyes and promises of getting together soon. Heartfelt goodbyes and promises that were never meant to be kept. The house was empty of friends and strangers now and only family sat solemnly around the dining room table. Pa's chair stood sadly empty at the table's head. Mother had brewed a fresh pot of coffee. There was plenty of food left over but no one had much of an appetite. The adults drank their coffee in an uncomfortable silence that was finally broken when Dad announced that we had better start our journey home.

I crawled into the back of the station wagon and claimed the seat next to the window. As we pulled away from the curb, I could barely see the silhouette of my Nannie as she waved from the front door. Then, the door closed and she was gone.

The little white house on Herrick Street shivered in the cold night air.

Chapter Sixty-one

Herrick Street—in transition

In the weeks following the funeral, Uncle Joe and Tante, who had delayed their return to Chicago, drove Nannie to our house every weekend. Mom was concerned about her mother being all alone. But now they had to leave. Uncle Joe had a construction project that desperately needed his attention and Tante's kindergarteners were anxious for her to return.

Mother had promised that she would take me to Herrick Street on the upcoming Saturday as I was anxious to see my grandmother. Anxious in a good way because I missed her and anxious in a bad way because I was concerned for her well-being. Of course, I spoke to her on the phone and I knew that Freddie was right next door if Nannie needed anything and the women in the sewing circle had been alerted.

I morphed into pesky mode as soon as my eyes opened on Saturday morning. I rushed downstairs, seeking my mother out, as she stirred a skillet full of scrambled eggs on the stove. I gobbled down my breakfast and with the promise that I would wash the dishes and feed the cat if she would only hurry it up so that we could leave for Elmira. We were in the car by ten o'clock and pulling up in front of Nannie's house an hour later.

Something looked different. I couldn't quite put my finger on it and aside from the venetian blinds being tightly closed, there wasn't anything else, visually, that had changed. I was nervous, uneasy in a queer way.

Once inside, there was nothing that might alleviate my fears. This was definitely not the Herrick Street that I was familiar with. The rooms were dark and dingy in stark contrast to the time of day. Mother turned on the two table lamps in the living room but dusk prevailed.

The most unsettling of all, was that there were no smells in the house. There was not a hint of a pot roast or an apple pie or a pot of coffee or burned toast that had stayed in the toaster just a bit too long. Even the refrigerator begged to be opened and when it was, there was nothing inside except for a row of lonely condiments, a hunk of cheddar cheese, and a dried-up loaf of Sunbeam bread.

This just could not be my grandmother's fridge that was always bulging with delicious stuff to eat. Where were the three tins filled with the trilogy of puddings, butterscotch, chocolate and tapioca? Where was the leftover chili or the rest of the baked chicken from Sunday's dinner? Where were the veggies and salad stuff, the bowl of applesauce and cold mashed potatoes? There were no pies cooling on the counter. The cookie jar was empty, except for the sad remnants of crumbs that clung to the bottom.

As soon as we were back in the car for the trip home, my observations poured out. A tsunami of concerns and an avalanche of worries. Like water gushing from a broken water pipe, an open fire hydrant, I babbled on and on about the empty refrigerator, about how gloomy everything seemed, and weirdly enough, how I felt chilled even though I could hear the furnace running. To my surprise, Mother nodded in agreement and confirmed that she had indeed felt the same way and that she had similar concerns.

But what were we to do? Nannie was grieving over the loss of her husband and we couldn't do anything about that. Nannie had been married to Pa for a gazillion years and now he was gone. We couldn't do anything about that. Nannie was not used to being all by herself and she was very lonely.

We could definitely do something about that.

Chapter Sixty-two

Life Again on Herrick Street—a furry friend saves the day

The hunt for the perfect companion for my grandmother was on as soon as we got home. Nannie was lonely and a pet would give her something to care for, something to fuss over, something to love.

We shared our concerns and our plan for resolution with Dad and he thought that a pet was a great idea. At first, we talked about getting Nannie a dog. She had always loved dogs. She was most assuredly a dog person, but dogs were a lot of work. They had to be walked and brushed and bathed and Nannie was becoming quite frail. Maybe a dog would be too much for her.

It was suggested that maybe we should get her another parakeet. She had one in the past, his name was Billie Bird and she was crazy about him. However, things did not work out so well for Billie Bird. It was unfortunate, but Nannie knew little about parakeets. When he began to molt, she thought that he had some terrible disease and rather than watch him suffer, she decided to end it all by putting him in the oven with the gas on. That was the end of Billie Bird's suffering.

That was the end of Billy Bird.

What about a cat? Nannie had never had a cat, but they were easier to take care of than a dog and more company than a bird. And they didn't molt. It was decided. A cat would be the perfect pet.

Now if anyone knew of a kitty that needed a good home, it would be Patty, the telephone operator. Patty was the one that had found our cat Missy for us. All Mom had to do was pick up the receiver. It was that easy. Now it just so happened that Patty had been chatting with Mrs. Lawrence, who was the wife of the local veterinarian. Mrs. Lawrence just happened to have heard about a woman in Burdett who was moving into a nursing home and couldn't take her beloved Siamese cat with her. She was heartbroken and was desperately looking for a new home for him.

Worry no more. Nannie will love him.

The next time we made the trek to Nannie's house, she had had her new kitty friend for a little more than a week. I was hoping that our plan was working and that I would see a difference when I got to Herrick Street. Straight away, I noticed that the front blinds were no longer closed and Nannie actually had the front door open and she was waiting for us. What a relief!

I jumped out of the car and raced onto the porch. As the front door swung open, I was greeted by the most handsome cat that I had ever laid my eyes on. He was gorgeous with perfect seal point markings, beautiful green eyes, and the unmistakable meow that could only belong to a Siamese cat. His name was Ramu. Nannie explained that the previous owner had named him after some ancient Siamese ruler that she had discovered in her Encyclopedia Britannica. The name seemed to fit.

Inside the house, the change was palpable. The chill was gone. The dark gloominess was gone. There was sunshine streaming in all the windows.

There was something to smell, an odor that greeted me at the door. Not the chocolate chip cookies that I was hoping for, but the foul smell of fish. There was an enormous pot of cod, boiling on the stove, that Nannie had procured from the fishmonger. Thankfully, this was not going to be our lunch, but supper for the cat. He dined on a china plate on a holiday placemat that my grandmother carefully positioned on the narrow kitchen counter.

This was one lucky cat and the ideal companion.

Chapter Sixty-three

A Close Call—Nannie living alone

There were happy times, once again, on Herrick Street. Ramu ruled the roost, living the life that most felines only dream of. On sunny mornings, he could be found sprawled across the floor, soaking up the sunshine that warmed the upstairs hallway. He spent his afternoons prowling amongst the hydrangea bushes, in the garden, doing what cats do and at night he curled up with Nannie wherever she happened to fall asleep. He sat on her lap, wrapped in the folds of her apron, as she rocked away tepid afternoons on the front porch and protested loudly if supper was running a bit behind schedule. And for all this royal treatment, all that Ramu had to do was to be a cat. It was as simple as that.

Nannie was adjusting to her new life. Life without her husband. She had been sleeping better and if she did wake in the middle of the night, she would stretch her arm out into the darkness until she touched something warm and furry and fall quickly back to sleep. She was finally getting her appetite back after weeks of not feeling the least bit hungry. The refrigerator was once again filled with good things to eat. Pie crust was rolled out on her pastry cloth, apples were peeled, sugar cookies filled the cookie jar, and butterscotch pudding bubbled on the stove.

There was the weekly meeting of the women in the sewing circle. Thursdays at one o'clock sharp. It was on one particular Thursday, that Nannie decided to make a quick lunch before the girls arrived. There would be plenty of time to cook up a hamburger, munch it down and then tidy up before one o'clock. There was a package of ground round that she had picked up from Karam's meat market that would make the perfect burger. The patty sizzled in the cast iron skillet until it was medium rare and then plopped on top of a sesame seed roll, crowned with a slice of sweet onion and then drowned in a bath of pickle relish.

At one o'clock, the entire sewing circle had gathered on the front porch. They rapped on the front door, at first softly, but no one came. They then knocked with more force, with more determination. Harder and harder until the door rattled at its hinges. But still no one came to the door. One of the women pressed the doorbell and although they all could hear it echoing through the house, no one came to the door.

By now, everyone was becoming quite concerned. They peeked through a slight opening in the curtain that hung in front of the picture window, behind the swing, but nothing. Nothing was out of place, nothing out of the ordinary and yet still, no one came to the door.

The most adventurous of the group, Florence, decided to walk around to the side yard and see if she could get a look through the kitchen and dining room windows. Nothing in the kitchen. So, it was on to the dining room, where on tippy toes, she peeked over the windowsill. Her worst fears were realized as she stared at a motionless heap next to the dining room table. Her screams brought Freddie out of the house next door and in tandem they pushed through the screen on the back porch and were inside.

Within a matter of just a few minutes, an ambulance was parked at the curb and medics in white coats huddled over my grandmother. They had pulled a large chunk of hamburger from the back of Nannie's throat. Now, thank goodness, her coloring was no longer a squidish, purplish gray. Her breathing was getting back to normal and although her blood pressure was a tad scary, she assured them that she was just fine.

She had sewing circle with her friends and she was already late getting things underway.

Chapter Sixty-four
Plan B—Mother takes charge

Somehow, Mom found out about the choking episode; the ambulance, the sewing circle women in a panic, Freddy breaking in through the back door, and Nannie unconscious on the floor. She was not at all pleased that her mother had somehow forgotten to mention the incident. Maybe she and Tante had been too quick to acquiesce to Nannie's insistence that she would be just fine living alone on Herrick Street.

A week later, my parents picked up Tante and Uncle Joe at the airport. A family meeting was scheduled in order to tell their mother of their concerns and share with her a plan that had been concocted, on the phone, several days prior.

The meeting took place around the kitchen table at our house. Adults only, as I was shooed out of the room. I left reluctantly, but I didn't go far. I crouched on all fours in the hallway on the other side of the kitchen door. Nannie sat quietly as the meeting began. Mother went first, taking on the role of the young matriarch. She was firm but reassuring. Tante was supportive of whatever her sister was saying and relieved that Mother had taken charge. Dad tried to put a less serious spin on all this and Uncle Joe recounted an experience that he had with his own mother. I listened as everyone said their piece and now it was Nannie's turn.

She admitted that the choking incident had really given her pause and although she was adjusting to living alone, the truth of the matter was that she really didn't want to be all by herself. In the end, she had much to consider and only she could make the final determination.

The decision to leave Herrick Street would not be an easy one. The house had been built for Nannie's grandmother around the mid-1800s and had been in the family for generations. Babies of the clan had been born in the upstairs back bedroom and old timers had been laid out in the parlor, just inside the front door.

My grandmother had inherited the house when she and Pa were married. They had raised their children there, entertained family and friends there, put up fifty- three Christmas trees there and planted countless tulip bulbs in the garden, next to the garage.

There was way more at stake here than just plaster and clapboard. There were memories that lived in the walls like ghosts that had escaped from the family picture album. There were creaky floorboards and windows that shimmered with hundred-year-old glass.

There was a tiny claw foot tub in the only bathroom and an old furnace in the cellar that Pa stoked, with shovels full of the blackest coal, to keep the house warm in the depths of winter.

There were little things like the decades old calendar that hung in the dining room, with a picture of the benevolent face of Christ. His hair and beard were all aglow with a celestial halo of light.

On the back porch, stood her old wringer washing machine that she hadn't used for years but just couldn't seem to part with. There was a collection of vintage stoneware sauerkraut crocks that had belonged to her mother. There were smaller crocks for pickles and shelves lined with empty mason jars, ready for the upcoming summer's crop of tomatoes and rhubarb that she grew in the backyard.

No, this was not going to be easy leaving her house, her friends, her flower garden. Not easy leaving Herrick Street, the Methodist Church that she had attended for years, her neighborhood. But maybe it was time.

And so Nannie agreed that it would be in her best interest if she sold Herrick Street and moved to our house in Watkins Glen.

The decision was made.

Chapter Sixty-five
The Preparation Begins—much to be done

The timing could not have been more perfect. For years, Harriet and Jim Fasio had lived in a cordoned off upstairs section of the house and now they were moving.

It was an adorable little space with its own entrance right off the street. Nannie would love it. She could come and go as she pleased, make her own meals in her tidy little kitchen and there was a door in her bedroom that led right into our hallway upstairs. She would still have her independence, but it would be under the watchful eye of my mother.

This was also an ideal arrangement for my parents. Fewer trips to Elmira for visits, fewer worries about Nannie's well-being and safety. Was she eating properly? Was she warm enough or cool enough? Was she feeling well? Had she fallen and there was no one there to rescue her? And on and on and on.

I could tell that Mom was excited by the prospect of having her mother so near, of being able to see her every day. No big deal, just an impromptu cocktail in the evening before dinner. Nannie was known to be quite fond of an occasional daiquiri in the summer or a touch of Irish whiskey on the rocks when it was frosty outside.

Although he never mentioned it, my dad's eyes would light up at the mere mention of Nannie's beef stroganoff or Swiss steak.

Of course, I was very excited about my grandmother living with us. I could just imagine every day hurrying up the hill after school, entering Nannie's apartment with a secret knock on the bedroom door and when invited inside, being greeted with the smells that could only come from my grandmother's kitchen. A devil's food cake begging for some seven-minute icing, peanut butter cookies, cooling on the counter. Yes indeed, I couldn't wait.

Before she could move in, there was much to do. Gallons of paint and buckets of wallpaper paste were stacked in the corner along with drop clothes and rollers and brushes in all shapes and sizes. Wallpaper was ordered for the kitchen, replete with perfect rows of tiny teacups and vines of swirling ivy. The kitchen also needed a new stove and refrigerator and there were places where the linoleum had pulled up and would have to be repaired. The rest of the apartment needed a fresh coat of paint. Paint on the walls, white semi-gloss on all the woodwork and doors, and the dingy ceilings could not be overlooked. There was material for curtain making that Mother bought at Posse's Five and Dime and Dad built bookshelves in the nook that was tucked in a corner of the living room.

The goal was that all would be ready by Thanksgiving. Tante was coming from Chicago to celebrate turkey day with the family and the following Saturday, it would be all hands-on deck for the big move.

Thanksgiving morning, bright and early, Mom and Dad did a final inspection on the apartment. It was ready. It was perfect. By ten o'clock Tante and Nannie arrived at the house, the backseat of the car piled high with a leaning tower of fruit pies, meringues, prune whip and vanilla pudding. A bowl the size of a small bird bath, filled to overflowing with twenty-four-hour salad, was wedged between the pie carriers. There were jars of sweet gherkins, pickled watermelon rind and ruby red cranberry sauce.

Mother had put the bird in the oven at the crack of dawn, the Candlewick dishes and serving pieces sparkled with expectation, and there wasn't an empty burner on the stove top, where all manner of deliciousness bubbled away. I was in-charge of the table setting, forks on the left, knife blades facing in, wine glasses and water goblet just so.

At two o'clock sharp, the family gathered in the dining room and the feeding frenzy began. Dad sliced the turkey and bowls of mashed potatoes and creamed onions and green bean casserole and stuffing circled the table like planets around the sun.

There was chatter and laughter and compliments to the chef. There were toasts and messages of thankfulness and happy whispers and loud guffaws. There were mountains of fluffy potatoes, with rivers of giblet gravy, pouring over the edge of every dinner plate.

After this gluttonous display of overindulgence, it was time for cleanup and dishwashing. My father hastily disappeared into the TV room, where there was a football game in progress. After all, clean up was women's work.

My sister and I cleared the table and stacked the dirty dishes on the counter next to the sink. Tante and Mom wrapped the leftovers in wax paper, carved the rest of the turkey from the carcass, scooped the potatoes and veggies into bowls and put the dessert; the pies and prune whip and pudding on the buffet table in the dining room.

Nannie donned an apron from the back of the pantry door and positioned herself in front of the steamy kitchen sink ready to do battle with the piles of dirty dishes, glasses and platters and greasy pots and pans.

At five o'clock I wandered back into the kitchen and found my poor grandmother still up to her elbows in dirty dishwater and Brillo pads. She looked exhausted. Her face was flushed, and a steady stream of perspiration washed over her round face. Her glasses were all foggy and her once meticulously quaffed hair lay flat and wet on her head. I begged her, "Let me help you. I can take over from here. You look so tired." She scoffed at the notion that she needed any help and instead invited me to sit at the kitchen table and keep her company. I was all too eager to oblige.

At one point, I noticed that she, very discreetly, reached into her apron pocket and pulled out a tiny white pill that she popped under her tongue. I noticed, but I didn't say anything, instead I queried to myself. What was that pill? Was my grandmother sick? Of course not. I had to put any such thoughts out of my head.

When every dish had found its way back into the cupboard, when every pot and pan was stacked neatly on the top shelf of the pantry, when the sinks were scoured and the dish towels were laid out to dry, Nannie joined me balancing a cup of coffee and a glass of milk in one hand and two pieces of chocolate pie in the other.

The perfect end to a perfect Thanksgiving.

Chapter Sixty-six
Close—and yet so far

Nannie had made an appointment with Dr. Hillman on the day after Thanksgiving for a quick checkup before the big move. She sat on the examining table, her eyes focused on one of the ceiling tiles as the good doctor listened and listened to her heart and then listened and listened to her lungs and then back to her heart.

Finally, he stepped back, wrapped his stethoscope around his stubby neck and announced that he had heard something that concerned him and that she needed an EKG. His office nurse called the hospital and set up an appointment for eleven thirty that same day. Tante would leave the doctor's office and take her mother straight to the Arnot Ogden where the tests were to be administered.

The results of the test were conclusive. The doctor's suspicions were confirmed. The EKG showed that Nannie had had a mild heart attack and that her heartbeat was still not normal. She had been diagnosed years before with angina but had paid little attention to the oft recurring sharp pain in her chest, except for an occasional popping of a little white pill. She was admitted to the cardiac floor at one o'clock in the afternoon and by one-fifteen we were in the car heading towards Elmira.

We huddled around the hospital bed as the matriarch of the family tried to reassure us that all these tests, all this poking and prodding was just a bunch of hooey...just a waste of time and that she felt just fine. But regardless of how much she insisted that she needed to go home, the doctor wasn't hearing any of it. After looking at the EKG, Mother agreed. Better to be cautious, better to be safe than sorry. There need not be any rush to leave the hospital. There was plenty of time for Nannie to move into her new apartment.

It had been a very long day and it was becoming more and more obvious that it was time for us to leave as Nannie struggled to keep her eyes open. One by one, the family said their goodbyes and filed out into the hallway. I was the last to leave, not wanting our time together to end. Stalling at the foot of the bed, pretending to be looking out the window. Mother poked her head in the door and announced that it was time to leave. I kissed my grandmother on the forehead. She opened her eyes just long enough to give me a sly little wink before I scurried out the door.

Frances Margaret Chamberlain Hewitt died at 12:06 AM on November 28th in room C12 at the Arnot Ogden Hospital in Elmira, New York.

Chapter Sixty-seven
The Dream—the end

Years later, when I was all grown up, an adult, a wife, a mother, I told my own children stories about their great grandmother. Stories about my Nannie and how she had such a positive influence on me.

I told them about their Orange Irish heritage, about intolerance in the name of organized religion. I told them stories about our family's odyssey from the Emerald Isle to the mines of Pennsylvania.

I read to them story after story. The same stories that Nannie read to me. So that they too would learn to value great writing and to appreciate the likes of Robert Louis Stephenson and Edgar Alan Poe and Beatrix Potter.

I cooked and baked for them recipes from the old country and from Nannie's dog eared, stained and yellowed Fannie Farmers Cookbook.

I told them about the dream.

It was dark, very late at night. There was no moon, no stars, only one lonely streetlight that was trying its best to light the way. I remember that I was walking on the sidewalk and the cracks in the cement looked eerily familiar. There were large trees, with deeply rutted bark, that stood like mighty sentries in the swale, next to the street. Large trees, that looked just like the elms, that had once upon a time, lined Herrick Street until the plague of Dutch elm disease had destroyed them all.

I glared into blackness trying to get my bearings, but to no avail. Suddenly, a porch light flashed in the distance, leading me up the sidewalk and onto a front porch. There was a rusty old mailbox with the faded numbers 413 hanging by one screw from the door jamb. My grandmother's address was 413... 413 Herrick Street.

Without thinking, I gave my secret knock on the screen door. It was the same secret knock that I wanted to use on Nannie's apartment door, but I never got a chance. I knocked again and again, no one answered the door. Disappointed and at the same time relieved, I turned to leave.

At that very moment, the door slowly opened, and a stream of light poured out onto the porch. I turned and there she was. My grandmother. My Nannie. The words tumbled out of my mouth. "Oh, my goodness. You're still alive. Why didn't you let me know that you were here? I could have had all these years with you."

Without warning, without any provocation, the door closed, the porch light flickered, and my grandmother was gone.

There I stood alone, all alone. Alone in the dark.

———————————